ITALIAN FILMMAKERS

Self Portraits: A Selection of Interviews

Jean A. Gili

ITALIAN FILMMAKERS
Self Portraits: A Selection of Interviews

Translated from the French by
Sandra E. Tokunaga

GREMESE

AKNOWLEDGEMENTS

The interviews presented in this volume first appeared in magazines. Some now include previously unpublished sections; others have been partially taken from my collections *Le Cinéma italien*. For clarity's sake and also to express my thanks to the publications concerned, the following is a list of the sources of the various chapters:

Bernardo Bertolucci: *Le Cinéma italien,* vol. 1, Paris, U.G.E., 1978, coll. 10/18. *Positif,* no.424, June 1996. (Interview conducted in collaboration with Christian Viviani. Numerous additions appear in the version published here.)

Mauro Bolognini: *Le Cinéma italien,* vol. 1, Paris, U.G.E., 1978, coll. 10/18.

Luigi Comencini: *Ecran 75,* no. 32, January 1975; *Ecran 76,* no. 43, January 1976, republished in *Le Cinéma italien,* vol. 1, Paris, U.G.E., 1978, coll. 10/18. *Ecran 79,* no. 80, May 1979.

Federico Fellini: *Positif,* no. 244-245, July-August 1981, republished in *Le Cinéma italien,* vol. 2, Paris, U.G.E., 1982, coll. 10/18. *Positif,* no. 300, February 1986.

Mario Monicelli: *Ecran 77,* no. 61, September 1977, republished and expanded in *Le Cinéma italien,* vol. 1, Paris, U.G.E., 1978, coll. 10/18.

Sergio Leone: *Positif,* n° 280, June 1984.

Dino Risi: Catalog *46ème Festival International du Film de Cannes,* May 1993.

Francesco Rosi: *Cités-Cinés,* Paris, La Grande Halle de la Villette, Editions Ramsay, 1987. *Ecran 79,* no. 83, September 1979.

Ettore Scola: *Cités-Cinés,* Paris, La Grande Halle de la Villette, Editions Ramsay, 1987. *Intervention,* no. 8, February/March/April 1984.

Giuseppe Tornatore: Press release for *The Star Man* published upon the release of the film in France (dist. AFMD), March 1996.

Front Cover Photo
From left to right: Bernardo Bertolucci, Sergio Leone, Federico Fellini and Giuseppe Tornatore.

Photo Credits
A.L.A. Fotocine: pp. 86 (below), 88 (above); Beer, Deborah: p. 27; Biciocchi, Roberto: pp. 90, 91; C.I.C.: pp. 107, 137; Cineriz: pp. 18, 72, 73, 131, 139; Ciolfi: pp. 9, 22; Consolazione, Ermanno: p. 104; De Laurentiis Cin.ca: pp. 15, 16, 34, 66, 78, 86 (above); Documento Film: pp. 64, 77; Filmauro: pp. 94, 95; Gaumont Distr.: pp. 110, 111; I.N.C. Distr.: p. 11; Incei Film Distr.: p. 84; Interfilm: p. 102; Lux Film: pp. 50, 65; Novi, Angelo: pp. 39, 138, 143, 150; Number One P.A.R.: pp. 105, 106; Paramount Pictures: p. 23; Patriarca: p. 80; Pennoni, Angelo: pp. 29, 55; Pierluigi: pp. 31, 49, 53; Poletto, G.B.: pp. 20, 21, 25, 83; RAI-TV: p. 135; Roma Press Photo: pp. 37, 40, 70, 87; Ronald, Huguette: p. 33; Schwarz, Angelo: p. 103; Strizzi, Sergio: pp. 108, 109, 112; Titanus: pp. 54, 71, 88 (below), 120, 123, 125, 126, 128; Tursi, Mario: pp. 98, 99, 154, 155, 160; Visentin, Guglielmo: p. 12; Vitale, Franco: p. 69.
Every possible effort has been made to give correct and detailed photo credits.
Obviously not all historic data has been easily accessible or necessarily precise. The author and publisher express their regret for possible errors or omissions and shall be glad to accept any authorized revisions, to be included in future editions.

Jacket design by Carlo Soldatini
Photolithography by Speed Art - Rome
Printed and bound by C.S.R. - Rome

© 1998 GREMESE EDITORE s.r.l., Rome
88, Via Virginia Agnelli - 00151 Rome, Italy
Tel. + 39-6-65740507 - Fax + 39-6-65740509
E-mail: gremese@gremese.com - Internet: www.gremese.com
ISBN 88-7301-149-7

CONTENTS

PREFACE

Interviewing the main protagonists involved in creating motion pictures and thereby, little by little, tracing the outlines of Italian cinema and the society from which it has emerged – the two being inseparable if we agree that the medium of cinema is an extraordinary revealer of a culture and a civilization – is part of a global undertaking. A collection of interviews is always a contribution to the history of a cinematography and to the knowledge of a society, a contribution whose basic method – oral history – is fundamental to any approach to contemporary phenomena. Moreover, cinema, a collaborative art par excellence, undergoes during its gestation and expression so many influences and interventions that it is always fascinating to return to the source and give directors a chance to clarify what their intentions were, describe the difficulties encountered, concessions necessarily made, their relationships with various collaborators, how they feel about their films once completed.

Thus the ten interviews gathered here are an opportunity to explore Italian cinema through the commentaries expressed by different voices, all of them illustrious and representative of trends, genres and periods that have marked the history of one of the world's most brilliant cinemas.

The most famous of all these filmmakers, the inspired magician of La Dolce Vita *and* 8 1/2, *Federico Fellini, is present, of course. A tireless storyteller, Fellini records his days as a youth, how he discovered cinema, and his strange rapport with Cinecittà studios where he notably chose to build the colossal sets for* Satyricon, Roma, Amarcord, Casanova, And the Ship Sails On...

Then Mauro Bolognini follows in his stride, certainly the most inspired Italian filmmaker when it comes to recreating the past. From a formal point of view, his success, on a par with Visconti, was also enhanced by the participation of set and costume designer Piero Tosi. The Love Makers, Metello, Bubù, Drama of the Rich, Down the Ancient Stairs, The Inheritance, La Venexiana – *are all a voyage in themselves through an Italy that has long since disappeared, but which we relive through the filmmaker's masterful style.*

The great maestros of Italian comedy, Luigi Comencini, Mario Monicelli and Dino Risi, demonstrate the art of observation and the capacity, through their unforgettable films, focusing in on the quirks and foibles of a society. As crucial witnesses of a country bursting under the pressure of its contradictions, they were also the moralists of a people faced with reconstructing the basic rudiments of life. And then, in a more bitter vein and perhaps more heavily charged with ideological commitment, Ettore Scola speaks of the Rome in which he grew up and where he first discovered cinema; the films which hallmarked his career as screenwriter, and later as director, from We All Loved Each Other So Much *to* A Special Day, *from* Down and Dirty *to* Le Bal.

In the political vein, which is so fertile in Italian cinema, we have the commentary of a director noted for his scrupulous determination: Francesco Rosi. Salvatore Giuliano, Hands Over the City, The Mattei Affair, Lucky Luciano *and* Christ Stopped at Eboli *are only some of the examples of a civic commitment always prepared to contribute to reflections on the state of society. Rosi also shows his distress at the dramatic transformation of his city of birth, Naples, ravaged by frenetic real estate speculation and organized crime – the* camorra *– a reigning force in the worlds of prostitution and drug trafficking.*

Sergio Leone brought a special international renown to Italian cinema with his westerns and gangster films. Once Upon a Time in America *is without a doubt the most in-depth and inventive European approach to a typically American genre.*

Discovered in the early sixties with the release of Before the Revolution, *Bernardo Bertolucci was carried to international fame by* Last Tango in Paris *and* 1900. *And, upon the im-petus of his great creative force, as confirmed in* The Last Emperor, The Sheltering Sky, Little Buddha, *he then felt a need to return to the roots of a harmonious Italy through the splendor of its Tuscan countryside in* Stealing Beauty.

Finally, to herald in the young developing Italian cinema and highlight the regional attachment of many directors, an interview with Giuseppe Tornatore with a focus on The Star Man *brings us a filmmaker of epic scope in his desire to depict a people and a land: Sicily.*

Certainly, Italian filmmakers have been, and continue to be today, witnesses of their time and magicians whose images invite us to reflect and dream.

Jean A. Gili

Federico Fellini

(FIRST INTERVIEW)

– In the early forties you first became interested in cinema by collaborating on various screenplays. Among them I believe the most representative were those written for Aldo Fabrizi, Avanti c'è posto, Campo de' fiori, L'ultima carrozzella. *There was something new in these films; conformity to productions of the time was being put into question.*

– My contribution to cinema was very limited. I was working as a screenwriter but without much conviction. I didn't even really know what our work was going to be used for. I collaborated on scripts and sometimes also on stories, but I was working for a typically Roman actor, Aldo Fabrizi, a man who had his own rather folksy vision of the city. Basically I only contributed my professional know-how to this work. At the time I was a journalist, I was working for *Marc'Aurelio,* a humorous twice-weekly publication, and really wasn't thinking at all about making films. The idea of being a film director was completely foreign to me – as if someone had told me I was going to be an admiral–the same lack of any identification with the profession or with that type of work whatsoever. I wanted to be a writer, I wanted to be a journalist. I thought perhaps I might write for the theater, for radio and maybe for films too, but I really never thought of expressing myself through images. And then, I really felt that I had none of the characteristics of a film director, it seemed to me that I lacked the kind of authority, that taste for tyranny, confidence, that decision-making ability to make a hundred, a thousand decisions a day. Really the authority... I felt these were qualities completely alien to me. When I sometimes went to a studio, asked by a director to change a dialogue or come up with a short scene to suit the caprice of some fanciful actor in an improvisational mood, I was always surprised, amazed – I simply couldn't understand how people could work in all that uproar, in that highly special

A portrait of Federico Fellini, the 'magician' of Cinecittà.

atmosphere. It seemed to me that a film troupe at work did everything except work – in fact, it was difficult for me to understand what they were really doing... I heard cries, some swearing, then I saw the director go over to an actor or actress, speak in a low voice, and all of these people standing around in that confused and disjointed bivouac – or rather it seemed to me that perhaps these people were involved in work that was so secret, so mysterious, that its true designs were beyond my grasp. So, I really never thought of becoming a film director.

I also lacked the aptitude, the gift of already seeing in a screenplay the images it suggested. My job was actually to make up sketches, stories, conceived theatrically or with that rather vulgar and slightly loutish humor which was typical of the newspaper I was working for, the *Marc'Aurelio.*

Nevertheless, that being the case, most likely almost absent-mindedly, and without a film director's specific point of view – perhaps just naturally, almost unconsciously – I was led to express myself with a rather caricatural vision, a vignette artist's way of seeing things.

To go back to Aldo Fabrizi's films, my contribution was very relative, even marginal: first of all, the stories weren't mine, nor were the characters. They were Fabrizi's whims and vague desires. The bus conductor in *Avanti c'è posto,* the fishmonger in *Campo de' fiori,* the coachman in *L'ultima carrozzella,* were little characters that Fabrizi brought with him from the stage, humorous figures that he transposed from variety theater or the *avanspettacolo* [popular low-brow opening shows, curtain raisers before a film, *Trans.*]. And me, I collaborated on the writing of the texts for some of these characters, when it came to depicting them on the stage or making a recording. But the stamp, the mold, the personality belonged to Fabrizi. I really don't know what film directors in those days really contributed to that Roman day-nursery, so affected, so conventional... since these directors were in fact people like Mario Bonnard or Mario Mattoli, they brought their craftmanship, a type of construction that, with relative ease and quite indifferently, used both the studio and the street.

– But don't you really think, nevertheless, that these films brought a new freshness to the stereotyped universe of the cinema of the time?

– I never saw those films again after that, I don't really know if there was something new about them. In any case, that novelty depended above all upon Fabrizi more than the screenwriters or directors. It was he who had this worship for portraying the real, an almost paralyzing worship. He always used to say, "Let's make life." In his own way, crudely, he was quite naturally inclined to portraying the things he saw around him; he tried to depict his own vision of the small world of common shopkeepers. So, instinctively, in an obscure way, the portrayal was one of poetic realism – though in the broadest sense of the word, and with a cadence, rhythm, perspective, not only ideological but nar-

rative too, that was always based on the segments, the patterns of the *avanspettacolo* sketches: there was always a tendency to indulge oneself, to close the scene with a funny line, with a gag. It was, I think, something whose force and limitations were rooted in the *avanspettacolo* sketch. At the time, this could have seemed novel since in those days Italian filmmaking was entirely dictated by canons of comedy that were very fixed, that is Hungarian... In short, Italian cinema did not exist. The famous "white telephone" cinema was perhaps an abstraction – certainly of interest as a historical or sociological document of a specific period, all abstractions can be useful to express something individual – it seems to me, though, that these films (and I'm being careful about what I'm saying since I never saw those films again after that) really had nothing in them. They were that kind of very weak thing – I'm not talking about Fabrizi's films, but about the other ones – which didn't even have that unsuspecting poetic or strange something, not even that surreal quality that is often born out of being forced to create a certain type of product, a particular kind of construction. Perhaps a few of Camerini's films had something...

– Certain of Poggioli's films too, I think.

– Poggioli was already someone who had his roots in literature; therefore someone who desired a greater cultural commitment, or at least an expressive one, and who drew from a certain body of literature.

It seems to me that the cinema of that era didn't have the insolent health of the cinema of street acrobats, fairground stands, of cinema made like that; nor was it even that product of fate, sometimes extravagant, which is sometimes born precisely out of a forced escape from reality or ideology. That cinema, it seems to me, had nothing which corresponded to any particular characteristic: it consisted of Galeries Lafayette [a department store, *Trans.*] films, assembly-line products without any other purpose than to entertain the public with the most inoffensive ramblings, the most...

– Don't you think that this lack of character might also have been the consequence of a powerful phe-

 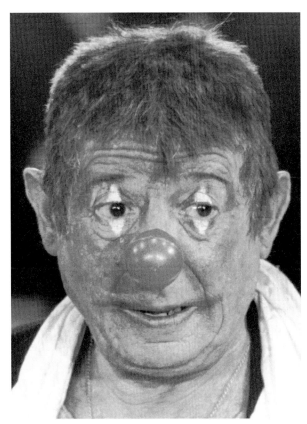

Portraits of circus clowns with warm faces for one of Federico Fellini's most personal films, *I clown/The Clowns*.

nomenon of self-censorship that affected filmmakers as well as screenwriters?

– Of course. Those of my generation came from a different type of background, from journalism, the *avanspettacolo*. Working in cinema was seen as a kind of Christmas present, a godsend: you earned much more in cinema than in any other field. In fact, I was always stunned when I received my advances for work on a script; they were always more than what I could make in a whole year as a journalist, probably even if I wrote night and day. And so I really don't know which one of us approached cinema as a form of expression. Certainly not me!

– *In those days, nevertheless, there were people like Cesare Zavattini who were beginning to work in films.*

– Yes, perhaps Zavattini... Yet what films of Zavattini's made during that period give evidence of any documentation, or even of one document, on the Italian reality? *Darò un milione* [I'll give a million] was nothing more than a little Molnarian fairy tale.

– *I was thinking rather of* Four Steps in the Clouds *by Blasetti.*

– But that film wasn't very Zavattian, the story was by Piero Tellini. But even that one... In those days French cinema was very popular, the French films of poetic realism, Carné, L'Herbier, Duvivier... I remember that we Italians were filled with admiration when we saw those films, those stories set in the underworld. For the first time prostitutes were shown... To us the French school of realism was truly exceptional. In our total ignorance, completely closed, we weren't capable of seeing the literary limitations of this cinema. It seemed to us, so locked up and separated from the rest of the world by the power of Fascism and the Church, that these stories really spoke of life. Our ignorance – I refer to my own ignorance at least, since probably sub-

Federico Fellini in Venice.

– The Little Martyr *by De Sica or* Ossessione *by Visconti are films from the years 1942-43. Here there was a real change in terms of the way you describe Italian cinema.*

– Yes, but already the war was upon us, there had been bombings. During 1940 to 1942, something happened that made Italians emerge a little from their bigotry. They started to feel that this security, this permanent Easter holiday, this vacation "on the coast" was leading to disaster. People saw the dead, the destroyed houses...

tler minds might have discerned something false in these films – was so great that these films mesmerized us: those streets, alleyways, fog, that desperate sense of life... To be quite honest, all of it was a bit strange to me, but of the two kinds of strangeness, between that of the "white telephones" on the one hand, and that of the "accursed hero à la Jean Gabin" conformity on the other, I felt I had a bit more sympathy for the latter.

Four Steps in the Clouds and other films, in a way, represented a tendency towards a kind of 'crepuscularism,' a certain decadence, to Pagnolism: the story of the incidents of daily life, trivial feelings, the boring routine of a gray existence. I even collaborated as screenwriter on *Four Steps in the Clouds* with Tellini. But it always seemed false to me. Today, I think I can say that that wasn't our reality. The reality of those days was that of *Amarcord – Amarcord,* yes, was a film that should have been made then, if we had had the awareness and the capacity to see ourselves with irony, detachment, and also with a little scorn. But I really must repeat that my idle chatter rather lacks generosity and is perhaps unfair: first of all, I really didn't go to the movies very often, and then, I never saw those films again after that.

– *You referred to your work as a journalist at* Marc'Aurelio. *What were the characteristics of this newspaper? What did it consist of?*

– The *Marc'Aurelio* was a humorous newspaper that grouped together a number of journalists from newspapers which Fascism had abolished such as *Il becco giallo, L'asino,* political and anti-clerical publications that supported a socialism somewhat à la De Amicis, and which Fascism had, of course, forbidden. So, many contributors to *Marc'Aurelio* came from other newspapers and wrote under different names: Otto Smith, for example, was Tomasino Smith who, after Liberation became director of the *Paese Sera* for many years.[1] Smith worked under a pseudonym, he even wrote texts for Fascist propaganda, he did this in fact right up to a year before the fall of Fascism. The group at

---

[1] Tomaso Smith, screenwriter from 1931 to 1943, founded *Il paese* and *Paese Sera* in 1947. He was director of the latter newspaper until 1956. In the late thirties and early forties, Tomaso Smith wrote several screenplays under the fairly obvious pseudonym Tommaso Fabbri (a clear indication of the attitude of Fascist censors who, as long as appearances were kept up, turned a blind eye).

Marc'Aurelio was very heterogeneous. Even some writers who held high posts in the Fascist hierarchy belonged to it, such as Celso Maria Garatti who wrote under the name Temisto and who was the chief of the Opera Nazionale Dopolavoro.[2] And then, there was the team of younger contributors, Steno, Benedetto, Ruggero Maccari, myself...

– Did the newspaper develop a satire of manners?

– Yes. Come to think of it, Giovanni Mosca in particular, consciously or unconsciously, was very inventive when he described situations or people, and had a parodic way of writing that was extremely caustic for those who wanted to delve into his deeper intent. On the first reading, Mosca's texts might only have appeared as somewhat abstractly humorous, a bit philological, surrealist, sentimental, whereas, on the contrary, some columns were cutting in their high parody. I remember one opening article in *Bertoldo* that was particularly revealing: Mosca speaks about a king who receives all his courtiers – courtiers in the broadest sense of the word, all eager yes men – in a text in which the intended satire is quite obvious. Nevertheless, most of these polemical moods, the disagreements, the revolt, not being able to be vented freely, found their expression in a sort of philological revolution, that is, in the absurd. There was a kind of rebellion in this, if not against conformity in general, at least against conformity in grammar, syntax, against the conformity of a certain type of scholastic literature. For example, again from Mosca's pen, we find De Amicis parodies and then, again, texts "in the style of" Carducci or D'Annunzio. And so, on philological, semantic points, a certain charge of revolutionary rebellion was let loose, but certainly it was very lukewarm.

– Because of the censorship, certainly satire had to be very indirect.

– Yes, but that being said, the censorship was extremely crude, stupid, as everything about Fascism. Even the censors could very well be fooled; they

---

[2] The "National Workingmen's Organization" was a state organization responsible for public recreational activities.

saw the most macroscopic things, the most obvious, but things that were slightly subtler, they didn't have the mental, cultural background to pick up. And then, at any rate, they were Italians...the Fascists didn't come from another planet. It was Italy expressing Fascism, and therefore with the same imprecision, the same underlying deceitfulness, the same attempt to find a balance between everything, even anti-Fascism – except, of course, in its extremes. But here I'm venturing into territory that honestly I don't know very much about. I wouldn't want a friend, furious, to stand up and prove my statements false.

So, I don't really think that there was true persecution. That eternal Italian mind, that old psychological crust – a thousand years old now – have produced the great balancing out of all things. The way of keeping everything suspended, of postponing until later; the long, slow periods of the Catholic Church – all of this existed already then. Nothing was ever really decided, since you "just never knew," since you could never be sure which way the wind would blow next, who would be the new boss. I think, in general, that apart from certain stupid fanatics' caprices of cruelty, savagery or folly, who intervened brutally, killed, or ordered a house arrest or imprisonment, that even under Fascism final judgements were usually always put off. Fascism wasn't Nazism, it was always something provincial, like a village fair... This was true to such a point that those journalists who had written for satirical anti-clerical and anti-Fascist newspapers, newspapers which had been abolished, nearly all went over to *Marc'Aurelio* and there, they continued writing under other names. All in all...

– Screenwriters also worked under pseudonyms.

– But of course. This Italian attitude can be seen in two different ways: on the one hand, as great wisdom, a form of Christian charity; and on the other hand, this same quality degenerates into a sort of deceitfulness, abjectness, and an inclination to the subtlest, most labyrinthine compromise – an aptitude for getting all kinds of possibilities to co-exist just to escape commitment, so as not to be forced to assume any ultimate responsibility. This is how we are, and we can see it in the absence of personal responsibility: there's always someone higher up. This can go right up to God Almighty. And so, you do whatever it is you're asked to do, but at the same time you also protect its opposite. This balance between debasement and the negation of debasement is a constant enjambement in which I really think the Italian, the Italian psychological type, can even give the best of himself.

– *Vito De Bellis, the editor of* Marc'Aurelio *was anti-Fascist wasn't he?*

– I don't believe he was anti-Fascist.[3] He was above all a true editor. In the extremely simplistic mentality that surrounded us, in the over-simplification to the point of intellectual impoverishment of any reference point as to what life really was, of any connection to life, De Bellis was an excellent editor. He had a flair for locating talented people, of course in a rough way, but with quite a good instinct. He knew how to intimidate them by creating an atmosphere as if we were in school, like the barracks. And we liked it. For my part, I feel a lot of gratitude to this editor. I think he's the only person in the world whom I still address in the formal *you* whenever I see him, so indelibly has the image of his authority been impressed in my mind, an easygoing authority, but all the same capable of imposing norms, limits, discipline. So, basically, when it comes to feelings, I remember *Marc'Aurelio* as friendly and protective, like a big, rather extravagant family, with lots of grandfathers just like the kind we would liked to have had when we were children–grandfathers who say four-letter words, who talk about "pussies" and "peckers," who make funny drawings. At *Marc'Aurelio,* there were grandfathers and fathers the way a youngster would want them to be. And so, a feeling of complicity grew up among us as among schoolmates; a big class allowed to do stupid things, better still, *paid* to do stupid things or to do anything at all against the lawful, the legitimate, against taboos. Nevertheless,

all within the rather juvenile limits of everything that was done in those days – a sweetened-up vision, simplistic, a little silly, a little stupid and, since it was stupid, also sometimes quite atrocious. Stupidity is always mean; and so, the mean side was always there, since meanness is expressed by stupidity.

– *It was beginning with* Marc'Aurelio *that you had your first contacts with cinema, wasn't it?*

– Yes, I started as a gag writer for Macario. Nevertheless, that collaboration was even stranger than the one with Fabrizi. We were given a prepared script that had been written by other *Marc'Aurelio* journalists, for example by Steno, who had also become Mario Mattoli's assistant. I don't remember if it was Macario or Mattoli who first said, "But why don't we have these scripts read by *all* the editorial staff and see if we can't add some more gags?" And this was how I became involved in my first screenplay called *Imputato alzatevi!* or... *Il pirata sono io.*

– *Chronologically, Macario's first film directed by Mattoli was* Imputato alzatevi!

– And so one day they gave us the script of *Imputato alzatevi!* with an advance that already seemed miraculous to us. Ruggero Maccari and I both got to work and, haphazardly, without the slightest concern for the scene's timing, wildly started sticking in quips, ideas, gags, with the same sort of witty comedy we used to create caricatures for the newspaper. They bought some funny lines from us.

– *When we see them today, those first films of Macario are still very funny.*

– I never saw them again. What those films needed was exactly what the contributors from the newspaper knew how to do, what they were trained to do, that is, writing puns, witticisms, surreal creations...

– *Besides those three screenplays for Fabrizi, you also collaborated on various other films during those years, for example, Alfredo Guarini's* Documento Z 3, *whose screenplay Zavattini also collaborated on.*

---

[3] In fact, in order to continue publishing *Marc'Aurelio*, De Bellis was forced to become a member of the Fascist party. Nevertheless, this membership should be understood in the context described by Fellini.

– Yes, with Zavattini, but there again it was a very peripheral collaboration. I'm not saying this to deny anything, I'm really saying it out of a concern to be fair. It was routine work, a detached collective effort, with very little personal involvement or enthusiasm – a text written for a newspaper, a drawing with your own signature done for a newspaper, is something that represents you, even if limited by your age, ignorance, inaccuracy, lack of real culture. Despite the adventurous "goliardic"[4] quality of your work, it is nevertheless something that you know how to do. Collaborating on films perhaps provided more excitement since there was less commitment.

– *We come across your name again on the screenplays of* Chi l'ha visto? *by Goffredo Alessandrini; of Nicola Manzari's and Domenico Gambino's* Quarta pagina; *and of Jean de Limur's* Apparizione.

– I don't remember *Apparizione* at all. *Quarta pagina* was an episode film. I wrote the story and screenplay with Tellini of *Chi l'ha visto?* I worked on lots of films as writer of stories and screenplays. I wrote a lot with Tellini, just the two of us. But don't ask me the titles, I really can't remember. I collaborated on a number of screenplays during that period – ten or twelve a year – many without any screen credit. We also worked as ghostwriters, wrote screenplays for others who claimed to be the authors.

– *I thought that with Piero Tellini you were given the chance of writing screenplays that were a bit more personal.*

– Yes, but it was always limited to the written word. There was never, I don't think, the slightest idea of what cinema was really about, of the meaning of the image. I remember that when I used to go to see these films, they never resembled at all what I had imagined while writing. I could hear the actors speaking the lines that I had created, yet the faces of the people saying them had no connection with those I had imagined. The situation, the lights... it

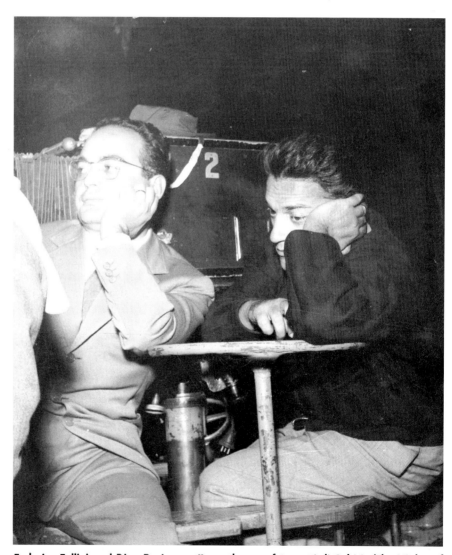

Federico Fellini and Dino De Laurentiis on the set of *Le notti di Cabiria/The Nights of Cabiria.*

---

[4] "Goliardic" is an adjective that describes the types of jokes and tricks students play.

Cabiria's 'colleagues' at the Baths of Caracalla in Rome, from *Le notti di Cabiria/The Nights of Cabiria.*

was always something else, a vague resemblance to the images I had evoked while writing, or vice versa, the images that had given birth to the theatrical writing.

– How did you go on to more significant work, one that made you feel you were involved in the creating of a film?

– The changes in my life – for me, I have never really understood them very well. The way I see it, there was never an act of will, of being conscious of what was happening. It seems to me that I have always been put before things after they've been accomplished, or at least when it comes to those things that have taken a tremendous importance in my life, that have been identified with my life: just like that, absent-mindedly, by pure chance. This is even how I feel about having become a film director. After my encounters with Rossellini and Pinelli, I started working more seriously as a screenwriter. The postwar years gave birth to several screenplays. That period was a renaissance in every sense of the word, but you, you are referring to the time before that, therefore... after the war there was greater commitment; after *Open City,* cinema became more serious.

– *Was it during* Open City *that you met Rossellini?*

– No, I knew him already. I had met him at the ACI, a film company directed by Mussolini's son, Vittorio Mussolini. I was part of the stories department and at the same time was working at *Marc'Aurelio.* They even sent me to Africa to go over a screenplay of a film entitled *Gli ultimi Tuareg.* I don't think the film was ever finished: the English soldiers of the 8th Army advanced, and the shooting was interrupted. In a way, it was fortunate that it was interrupted.

– *Could you tell me more about the circumstances of your trip to Africa?*

– It was an unforgettable adventure, a dream. I was at ACI, had a salary, was a stable employee in the company, as part of the stories department. I was supposed to read stories, books, make suggestions, go over screenplays, write some. It was full-time work and I even had hours; though I went in very little since I was still working at *Marc'Aurelio,* nevertheless I had a schedule. It was during the time I had avoided the draft by benefiting from a military discharge. This discharge was thanks to corruption in part, and also to my poor health. Also, I was enrolled at the university, was a journalist, a whole series of justifications that became more and more tenuous as the military situation worsened. Then, one day Vittorio Mussolini told me, or perhaps had someone else tell me, that I had to fly to Tripoli to help get a screenplay off the ground. I had absolutely no desire to go; moreover, at the time I was very much in love with a fantastic soubrette; I didn't want to leave her. But because of my military status, the matter was then presented slightly as blackmail, a threat: if I didn't go to Libya, the convalescence permission I had been granted to avoid the draft risked running out and I might be forced to leave for who knows where – Albania, Greece, Russia. So, I set off against my own will really, with the impression of having suffered an act of violence.

When I arrived, I settled into my hotel in the midst of bombs falling from the sky and canon blasts from the sea, and also from the land: the 8th Army was advancing... I settled into that deserted, chaotic hotel. Sometimes I went to join the film crew shooting in areas difficult to reach, near the edge of the desert. Strange film – one which I knew nothing about: *Gli ultimi Tuareg,* based upon a book by Emilio Salgari *I predoni del Sahara* [The robbers of the Sahara]; the screenplay, the situations, Osvaldo Valenti and Luisa Ferida [both executed by the partisans in April 1945 for their connections with the Republic of Salò, *Trans.*]... One night while I was following the making of the film, we had a sandstorm, the *simoun.* It was an incredible experience. We were all told to run for protection under some big tents. There were Arabs giving orders with circus cries, all of them extremely worried. And so we stayed there, our faces in the sand, under the tents, with the furious howling of the wind for an hour, an hour and a half. When we could hear the shouts of the Arabs again, who had directed the operations – a strategy consisting of hiding under the tents, our bodies pressed one against the other – we emerged. The landscape had completely changed: over here, where the flat horizon had been, there was now a mound; over there, where a hill had once stood, there was nothing. The truck was nowhere to be seen. Everything was buried under the sand, really just like a dream.

Unexpectedly, all the film crew was asked to immediately leave Libya since the civil airlines were no longer running. The crossing of *mare nostrum* – which was no longer ours – had become extremely dangerous there. A ridiculously dramatic scene then ensued, like in a bad movie: we drew lots between us to decide who would leave. The last civil aircraft – I think it was LAI[5] at the time – only had 40 seats. Franco Riganti, the film's director of production, had a taste for melodramatic scenes, that sort of heroic drama. The draw took place at night, each person having written his name on a piece of paper. At the last minute, overcome by who knows what kind of bizarre caprice, or perhaps under the influence of the pervading atmosphere there, I declared that I wasn't

---

[5] Probably this was in fact the airline Ala Littoria S.A.

Federico Fellini and his alter ego, his actor-mirror Marcello Mastroianni, during the days of *8 1/2.*

leaving: "I want to give my place to someone who has a family, to someone married." And in fact I refused to put my name in among the others – as at the lottery – in the colonial hat. The elevator boy of the hotel, an Arab youth with large eyes, was given the responsibility of drawing the lots and reading the names: up to forty. The names that remained in the hat would stay behind. Anyway, I had dropped out; Luigi Giacosi, who later was my director of production for *The Loafers* and *La Strada* (GB *The Road*), remained with me, and the actor Guido Celano stayed behind, too. We stuck together, the three of us, filled with a sense of adventure. Who knows what we were thinking. We thought the English would be coming; we never imagined that they might take us prisoner, we thought that our act of heroism would win the recognition of the Chief of the 8th Army, Montgomery. In my fantasizing, I even imagined myself in a personal meeting with Montgomery... Usually we were almost always drunk. Fear of the bombings, the solitude, the fact that we were often forced to take shelter in the cellar of the big hotel, the presence of Osvaldo Valenti who probably even then already had a taste for certain kinds of stimula-

tion under drugs, all of this produced a sort of giddiness and freed our fantasy and imagination. After three days, we too were starting to think of going back to Italy. By selling the carpets, silver bracelets that we had bought with our per diem for expenses, we found two Germans who accepted, in exchange for the money, to take us to Sicily in a small army aircraft. We made this return trip flying two meters above the deep in order to blend with the sea. A flying fortress accompanied us; we could see it at an altitude of 20,000 meters with a big white star on its underside. Perhaps it hadn't seen us. We made this trip in a plane that was about one-fourth the size of this room, sitting on the floor of the cabin, jolted about with two Germans, one at the control stick, the other with a machine gun constantly pointed at the flying fortress. And that was how we arrived in Sicily, at Castel Vetrano, right in the midst of the bombings. It was really hell: we got out of the plane and ran for cover.

– *I read in the magazine* Cinema *that* Gli ultimi Tuareg *was supposed to have marked the beginnings of actor Osvaldo Valenti as film director.*

– I don't really remember. The director was Gino Talamo, a man with big, very gentle eyes, who had also been an actor. Later, another director was sent to work with him, someone called Barboni. He was from America and only because he had lived for a while in the States – who knows what he did there – he enjoyed special authority. Italians who have lived in America come back speaking rather broken Italian. So, this Barboni always used to say, "How do you say – in Italian?" We really couldn't figure out how this man from Sora, De Sica's town, could all at once have forgotten how to say this or that word... Later Franco Riganti also stepped in as a self-styled director. So here were three people to direct the film: it was a good thing that the war came to make all three run away. Of this filming I especially remember Guido Celano who, wrapped in a large sheet – he played the part of an Arab traitor – was supposed to imitate the howl of a jackal. This was something that made us die of laughter, first of all watching how hard it was for Celano to walk in the sand with his big sandals, and then, he would keep getting his feet tangled up in the sheet, and finally because at night he had to go to the edge of a dune to create a silhouette that stood out from the sky against the light. And there, following the instructions the three directors had given him, he had to howl...

To return to your question, I don't think Valenti participated in the directing of the film; he only acted in it. Luisa Ferida was also there and was already pregnant, the poor thing, tired, exhausted... a situation of glorious disaster, of total collapse. It was the end of everything in a mocking way: there we were, making a film with Guido Celano howling at the moon, imitating the cry of a jackal... [6]

– *It was at the ACI, then, that you met Roberto Rossellini?*

– That's right. Rossellini was at the ACI, I saw him leaning out a window of the office next to mine. I heard someone talking, I went to the window, too, and saw a fellow looking down, with this sharp nose, this chin... He was talking to someone out on the street. We looked at each other, neighbors, like two people at two windows of a train, we started chatting, afterwards he came over to my office. And that's how I met him.

– *Do you believe that your encounter with Rossellini was something very important?*

– In terms of cinema, yes. Suddenly I realized that you could make films with the same lightness, the same freedom of expression as writing or drawing. The whole technical machine, all that logistical apparatus, had always paralyzed me since I thought it

required such commanding authority and also a commanding voice, everything I felt I lacked. Most of all, I didn't feel I had the right voice to be a director, to shout, to swear. But then with Roberto, as I half-heartedly followed the shooting of *Open City* – I used to sometimes go, with Sergio Amidei, to see him on the set, but I was always unattentive, detached, I kept a lot of distance – and of *Paisan*, my attitude towards cinema changed. For the film *Paisan,* I accompanied Rossellini not as assistant director but as traveling screenwriter. The film turned out to be a fundamental experience for me. First of all, it was the discovery of my own country: before that, the only times I had actually seen anything of it were sometimes standing at the window of the slow local trains I took to Calabria or Puglia while traveling with a revue troupe. Apart from Rimini or Rome, I didn't know much else, I didn't know Italy at all. I had spent a day in Naples once, but I hadn't understood a thing. However, with *Paisan* – that trip with the crew for the shooting of it – to Naples, all of the Amalfi coast,[7] Rome, Florence, and then right up to the Po – a total experience, lived day in and day out with intense feeling, constant excitement... particularly with *Paisan*, I discovered that cinema could aspire to the same personal expression as writing. The expressive 'conditionings' that had always seemed to me so invincible, were surmountable: with cinema you could really choose an adjective, give rhythm to a sentence... I saw Rossellini filming in complete freedom in the midst of a broken Italy. I have the text here of a book that Einaudi is going to publish; talks, discussions I've had sometimes in a rather unplanned way. Would you like me to read the passage about the shooting of *Paisan*?

– *Certainly.*

– "I went on the set to change situations or lines. It really amazed me that the director could maintain

---

[6] A strange reminiscence of this howling was that of Anita Ekberg's in *La Dolce Vita*, at night, in the surrounding Roman countryside, as she and Marcello Mastroianni ran away together.

[7] The first episode of *Paisan*, the one that is set in Sicily, and the fifth, set in Romania, were in fact shot in Maiori not far from Amalfi.

a detached relationship with the actresses. It was difficult to write dialogues in that confusion. I suffered terribly from the malaise of collective work; all together doing one thing, talking loudly. But it finally ended up that I couldn't work very well unless there *was* confusion, just like when I was a journalist writing articles at the last minute in the chaos of the editorial office. I felt more comfortable with films shot on location, outdoors; in this, Rossellini was really one of the first. The experience with Roberto, traveling with *Paisan*, was my discovery of Italy. Until then, I had never really seen much of anything: Rimini, Florence, Rome and a few small towns in the South glimpsed while I was traveling with the *avanspettacolo*; market towns and villages sealed in medieval night, like

those I had known in my childhood, only the dialects were different. I liked the way Roberto made films, like taking a nice trip, going out with friends. The good seed, I think, must have been this. By joining Rossellini during the shooting of *Paisan*, I suddenly realized very clearly – a joyous revelation – that you could make movies with the same freedom, the same lightness as when drawing or writing – making a film, enjoying and suffering, day after day, hour after hour, without worrying too much about the final result – that the same secret relationship, anxious and exalting, which one has with one's own neuroses; that the obstacles, the doubts, the after-thoughts, the tragedies, the exhaustion wasn't very different in the end from the painter's suffering as he searches for a tone on a

The woman temptress at the heart of Federico Fellini's universe. The director on the set of *Giulietta degli spiriti/Juliet of the Spirits*.

Already the echoes of the circus, Sandra Milo, provocative horserider and Lou Gilbert, in Federico Fellini's *Giulietta degli spiriti/Juliet of the Spirits*.

canvas, or the writer's when he erases and rewrites, corrects and begins again, in his search for the expressive sense, impalpable and evasive, that lies hidden among a thousand possibilities. Rossellini searched, he pursued his film in the streets, with the Allied tanks passing a meter from our backs; people shouting and singing at their windows, the hundreds of onlookers trying to sell us something or trying to steal something from us; in that glowing pot, that swarming lazaret which was Naples. And then Florence and Rome, in the endless marshes of the Po with problems of every kind, last-minute refusals of filming permits, programs cancelled, money mysteriously disappearing in the infernal round of improvised producers ever yet

cleverer, more infantile, lying, adventurous. Thus I feel I received from Rossellini an education that was never translated into words, never made explicit, never defined in a program; that I was taught the possibility of walking balanced among the most unfavorable conditions, the most annoying; and at the same time, with the natural capacity of knowing how to turn adversities and obstacles to one's own advantage, transforming them into a feeling, an emotional value, a point of view. That's what Roberto was doing: he was living the life of a film like a marvelous adventure to be simultaneously lived and told. His surrender with regard to reality, always attentive, clear, fervent; his way of naturally placing himself at an impalpable and unmistakable

The mediocrity of provincial life, the irresponsibility of juvenile adults. Jean Brochard and Franco Fabrizi in Federico Fellini's *I Vitelloni/The Loafers.*

point between the indifference of detachment and the awkwardness of belonging, allowed him to capture and to fix reality in all its spheres, to see things simultaneously from the inside and the outside, to photograph the air around things and to reveal that surprising, insatiable, dodecaphonic, mysterious, magic; something which is life. Isn't neorealism perhaps all of that? Which is why, like an admirable syllogism, when we speak of neorealism we cannot but refer to Rossellini. The others made realism, "verism," or tried to express a talent, a vocation, in a formula or a recipe. And even in his last films, in those made when he had received an advance or because... But now I'm talking too much about Rossellini."

– One last question: at the end of the war, how did you get together again with Rossellini and Aldo Fabrizi for the making of Open City?

– Rossellini came to see me at the "Funny Face Shop," the caricatures arcade. As for me, I had no intention of getting involved in cinema since I was earning a good living doing caricatures. Rossellini wanted to shoot a documentary from a short screenplay written by Alberto Consiglio about the life and death of Don Morosini, a priest who had been shot by the Nazis. He came to see me because I knew Fabrizi well, and wrote texts for him. In those days Fabrizi was acting in comedies at the Sala Umberto, sketches, topical farces, but always topics with a popular slant, stories about the black market, small-time traffickers... Rossellini wanted me to persuade Fabrizi to accept the role of Don Morosini. Roberto also had another project; he wanted to make a movie about the street urchins of Rome during the war. While we were all talking about it – Sergio Amidei was there, too – we thought of combining the two projects.

I collaborated on this film without much conviction. I remember that Sergio and I wrote the screenplay in a few nights, very quickly. The war wasn't over yet, it was still going on in the North.

(SECOND INTERVIEW)

– What do you think of when you hear the word "Cinecittà?"

– I can tell you what came to mind the first few times I heard that word. Something really fantastic, as if you had asked a doctor, or someone who wanted to become a doctor, what the word "clinic" or "hospital" meant to him, or if you asked a child with a religious vocation what "the Vatican" or "Saint Peter's Basilica" meant to him. When I was a child, that combination of syllables, the word Cinecittà, evoked probably in an obscure way the kind of city in which I wanted to live, a dimension that could become part of my own life. As far as seduction, of outward fascination, it was the city of movies and therefore the city of actresses, the city of divas. My generation had been born with the myth of American movies. All of us were fascinated by the Hollywood stars Clark Gable, Gary Cooper... For someone like me, who lived in a small provincial town, Rimini, just to know that in Italy there was Cinecittà too – that is, something that resembled Hollywood – was a source of great excitement, very seductive. And so, when I came to Rome to be a journalist, I was eighteen or nineteen years old, I always tried to get assignments to interview actors, film directors; in fact, just to go to Cinecittà.

I remember the first time I went there by streetcar, a little streetcar that from the station, from the city, crossed kilometers and kilometers of countryside running beside the ruins of a Roman aqueduct and then, finally, the appearance of a structure that, in fact, rather looked like a hospital, or the buildings of a university dormitory and yet bore the magic word: Cinecittà. I remember my excitement the first time I went inside, the doormen trimmed with braid with wide greatcoats like the doormen of big hotels and then, my first encounter with the great world of cinema.

I remember that Blasetti was there, with DIRECTOR all in capitals, who was filming I think, *The Iron Crown*. I had chanced on a very Italian film dimension: extras dressed as Romans of antiquity, large sets, colonnades, temples, marble staircases, a kind of home-made *Quo vadis?* a *Ben Hur* of Latium. And I saw in the midst of all the dust, of shouting extras, slaves, gladiators pulled by horses, I saw at one point, rising above this human tide, the arm of a crane that rose, rose, higher and higher, and there was a film director on the crane – the director in the expression of his greatest apotheosis, his most triumphant, covered with whistles, collimator viewfinders, megaphones, medals; with a visor, boots, a whip–and it was Blasetti, it was the film director who was ascending, rising up to the sun, into the clouds...

And then Cinecittà truly became my city. Often, when my journalist friends ask me what city I would like to have been born in, the answer comes quite naturally and I answer, "Cinecittà." It is the dimension most natural to me; the same thing, as I was saying before, as the hospital is for a doctor, the courthouse for a lawyer. If you don't stop me I can continue on like this, saying these silly things into infinity...

A winter of emotion along snow-covered roads. Anthony Quinn in Federico Fellini's *La strada/La Strada* (GB *The Road*).

An interview, a television program or...? Fellini, a world of writing, speech and thought.

something at Cinecittà for *I Vitelloni* too. It was born out of an expressive necessity. That is, by getting to know myself better and trying to express myself in a more personal way, it seemed to me – or rather, I was sure – that I could obtain the images that were in my mind in a more controlled way, with more rigor, in the studio.

Cinema consists of images, cinema is an image and we perfect the image with light, it is light that creates the image. In this way, I believe that cinema is closely related to painting, and therefore to light. In the studio we can command, control light, sculpt it, we can express ourselves with light; on location, this becomes more difficult. But apart from this fundamental problem of light, which is for me the most precious basic form of expression of cinema and of the film

– *In the first films that you shot,* The White Sheik, La Strada, *there were a lot of exteriors; then, little by little, the studio became more important until* And the Ship Sails On, *entirely filmed with artificial sets. How did the increasing importance of the studio develop in your work?*

– But even in *The White Sheik* there were sequences filmed at Cinecittà; all the back projections, for example, the entire ocean scene was done in the studio – I don't remember anymore which number it was – where the equipment for back projections was. I shot

image, there is also everything that concerns expression: the volumes, perspectives, the proportions of the things that must be expressed in a certain way, with certain details. To me the studio is the environment where the image seen in your imagination can be constructed by controlling everything, just as a painter does with his brush on canvas. He puts colors, tones, side by side, he takes into account distances, limpidity, perspective points. In the same way, sets can be constructed in a more rigorous way, with more pertinency to what we want to achieve. Because cinematographic expression is truly an artifice, a fiction, the tendency to make all films in the studio is normal. Artifice and fiction attain greater precision, plausibility, more faithfulness to the image of fantasy carried inside oneself.

– *Do you find it amusing making a plastic sea?*

– It's not a question of being amusing. I think that any expression fills its creator with a stimulating energy and it can therefore perhaps also be something fun. It's always a wonderful game, the marionette theater, shadow puppets, a way of painting, and of joyfully participating in the semi-divine activity which is creation. In this, there is the exaltation of oneself, of one's own ego... There is something very gratifying in this; it is the amusement of

the child when he plays. The plastic sea is an expressive necessity. The true sea is the true mother, she may show herself to be the least true of all because a specific feeling is missing. For *And the Ship Sails On* and for *Casanova* or for *Amarcord*, I thought that the sea too was an uncontrollable element.[1] If we want to give the sea a feeling – the

---

[1] With a little humor, we are led to believe that recreating an artificial sea might have been prompted by the difficulties encountered with the real sea during Fellini's shooting of *The White Sheik*. The director relates: "There is nothing more difficult or exasperating than having a camera on a raft in the middle of the ocean and trying to keep only the horizon and the blinding sun in view." (In *Federico Fellini*, "Intervista sul cinema," Rome-Bari, Laterza, 1983. French translation "Fellini par Fellini," Calmann-Lévy: 1984.)

How to take advantage of ignorance to rob your neighbor by disguising yourself as "Your Grace." Franco Fabrizi and Broderick Crawford in Federico Fellini's *Il Bidone/The Swindle.*

feeling of being a sea in a certain way – we can only do so with materials that will take lighting in a certain way until they can be charged, heavy with feeling. Apart from all the other problems related to the possibility of controlling ways of expression, the studio is the place that is the most protective; it is the structure best adapted to one's eventual surrender to the expressive plays of light, color, perspective, objects near and distant – in short, in evoking the world that we have imagined and making it materialize.

– *When you shoot in the monumental district of EUR in Rome, you treat it as if it were a studio set.*

– EUR suggests a vision of a metaphysical city, à la De Chirico, with those huge marble cubes, that linear quality. It is a district that has been drawn up on paper, an area that seems to have almost materialized "planimetrically" and at the same time it can also suggest some of De Chirico's cities, the green of the vegetation and the blue of the sky, the flat horizon and those volumes, those vertical structures. So, there is something set-like that suggests a studio construction, a movie set. In this way EUR can call to mind a set designer's visions. I've shot many exterior sequences at EUR; I even rebuilt this district in the *Boccaccio 70* episode... I almost rebuilt the whole area in miniature, a very large model in which Anita Ekberg had to appear huge: she was the projection of Peppino De Filippo's complexes of sexual inhibition, she was to move like a great divine goddess. We therefore reduced the proportions of the district so that she would appear colossal. I also filmed sequences of *La Dolce Vita* there. It was a neighborhood that fascinated me for this special decorative suggestiveness.

– *Working in the studio what kind of relationship do you have with the set designer, costume designer, the chief cameraman?*

– A tyrannical relationship, dictatorial, of total authority, "do what I say" [laughing]... an excellent relationship; they're friends. The set designer and the chief cameraman are the right and left hands of the creator; they are the fingers, the eyes. I have a relationship of ongoing close collabora-

tion; I express myself through them. In some cases they are even more important than the screenwriter. In the studio, something that existed only in the sphere of the imagination is made to materialize. Now we have to translate it into wood, iron, lights, colors, fabrics... Scribbling, drawing helps me a lot; I feel I can express myself with more pertinence, give my collaborators more immediate graphic and pictorial instructions, even to the cameraman. I've worked for a number of years with Peppino Rotunno; a relationship of great harmony, of great understanding has grown between us. In all of this work, there is the same relationship the painter develops with his paints, brushes, palette, lead white...

– *Your imagination, your fantasy find their natural form of expression in the studio and not on location.*

– Yes. For the kind of stories I tell, or I intend to tell, I feel I can be more precise – that nothing is left to chance, or to that impalpable factor, present in no matter what creative undertaking brought to the media by machines and a series of processes during which control becomes less rigorous: the laboratory, development, printing, copies... An entire series of operations come into play that can little by little denature, cool down, dilute the original idea. There is more control in the studio than being forced to depend on a constantly changing sunlight, which can never be controlled, despite all the reflectors or systems you might use to try to soften or heighten the light. This doesn't mean, however, that certain scenes shot in natural light can't faithfully represent what you've imagined, by trusting in your own chosen reality. Reality can also be worked, you can try to make it an expression closer to what you have imagined.

– *At the end of* And the Ship Sails On, *we are shown the camera, the studio. Is this a homage to Cinecittà?*

– A homage to Cinecittà? And if I had shot the film in another studio? It's not a homage to Cinecittà, it's a homage to cinema, to cinematic expression, it's also a way – at least this was my intent – to express my own point of view with a bit of modesty. Since the film's story might have expanded into a series of interpretations suggested by news events being lived at the moment, it risked being taken as an admonishment, an apocalyptic warning; so this camera that pulls back and reveals the studio, the artifice, the large mobile set on pistons that support it, the backdrops, all the crew, all of cinema's special effects – it was a way of saying, "As for me, I'm someone who makes films, and so I told this story, but I told it from my own point of view, as someone in entertainment."

There were several reasons I felt it was necessary to step back like that, to show the location where we were shooting. It was also a way of saying: "We're all in the same boat, even the author who pretends he's detached." The threat and the decision, the seeking of awareness, of understanding what's happening, also involves the person who is attempting to bring about this

Giulietta Masina and Marcello Mastroianni in Federico Fellini's *Ginger e Fred/Ginger and Fred.*

process. No one has an excuse, no one can find justification not to.

There was probably also another reason – which I say a little jokingly: I'm in love with the set, the

studio, behind the scenes, the lights, reflectors. So I wanted to reveal my means of expression, like a painter who might photograph his studio with its easels, canvases, palettes, rags... I, too, wanted to show the poor spectator, craving for realism, who during the viewing had eyed the plastic sea with suspicion, the vellum paper sun; I wanted to take him behind the scenes of the set and say, "Yes of course it's all artifice, fiction, look – it's total fiction in fact, but of such complexity, with such great machinery needed, that this is justification in itself."

– Don't you feel that the studio is somewhat a way of protecting yourself from the outside world?

– But no... since after all is said and done, a film crew is emblematic of society, of life outside. Everything can be microscopically reduced and at the same time represent the macrocosm, the universe. Life inside a studio, with all the problems of living together, is a true apologue of society, so it doesn't seem to me like I'm trying to protect myelf. That's something anyone can be accused of.

– It isn't an accusation.

– At any rate, this comment might also be made to a surgeon: "But you are always in the hospital operating, aren't you taking yourself too far away from life's problems?" Or the same goes for a writer, for anyone, even an astronaut: "By staying in space inside your space craft, aren't you forgetting the daily concerns of life a little?" It seems to me this question doesn't make any sense. Each person commits himself to what he knows how to do: by the path he has chosen, he works out his involvement and his problems.

Mauro Bolognini

– Perhaps before more general things, we can first talk about the main stages of your career. You got your start directing in 1953 with the film Ci troviamo in galleria. *Before that, you were an assistant to film directors such as Luigi Zampa and Jean Delannoy. And, as many Italian directors, you studied architecture before getting involved in cinema.*

– From architecture I went to the Centro Sperimentale di Cinematografia, but I was an auditor and not a regular student, so I didn't stay there long, only a year. And then I became Zampa's assistant. After that I worked for a while in France – there were co-productions – and I went to Paris as an Italian assistant. I worked on two films, one with Jean Delannoy, and the other with Yves Allégret. That stay was an important experience. I discovered a different way of making movies, completely different from Italian cinema. Those were the days when Italian cinema was in the throes of neorealism: it more readily braved the street than the studio, real characters more than actors. So for me, my experience in France meant going from non-professional players, or extremely simple, very genuine dialectal actors, to movies made with stars. For *The Moment of Truth* we had Michèle Morgan and Jean Gabin; for Yves Allégret's *Nez de cuir*, Jean Marais and Brigitte Auber. With these two films I got real contact with the studio, with a very professional way of working, without improvising. This was

very important for me, not because I liked one way of working more than another, but because I could enrich myself with an extraordinary experience which, in Italy at the time, was impossible. In fact, there they despised the studio, it was a era when working in the studio was definitely out. So, for me, this French experience was beneficial.

– When you returned to Italy you were Zampa's assistant on a very famous film, City on Trial.

– Yes, that was the last film I made with Zampa. After *Processo alla città* I started directing.

– Was it difficult to become a film director in the early fifties?

Based on a screenplay by Pasolini, young people tortured by existential malaise. Jeanne Valérie and Jean Sorel in Mauro Bolognini's *La giornata balorda/From a Roman Balcony*.

– In those days it would have been difficult if I had wanted to make *my* film; most probably very difficult. Nevertheless, that period was more open than today, simply because there were so many more productions, a tremendous number of films were being made. It was extremely hard to make your debut with a film that was very rigorous, to get big-budget producers to finance a personal movie; the only thing you could do was accept a commercial compromise. And that explains why my first movie was a commercial one, *Ci troviamo in galleria.* This gave me the experience of working with a whole line-up of actors: I had all the actors of the time, from Alberto Sordi to Carlo Dapporto, as well as many comedy players. I was working directly with them and, being in their midst, was able to try certain things out – with actors just starting out, for example, young people like Sophia Loren, who found herself among all of these veteran actors. So this film gave me a little niche where I had quite a free hand. I guess that was the positive side of the film, the winning of a little space for myself where I could work. I always believed in this possibility: with each film, I tried to make that space bigger and bigger. If in the beginning they told me, "You can only have one character to yourself, the others will be imposed by the producer, by commercial necessities, by public demand..." I would accept. I was happy just to have even one character to myself. In *Ci troviamo in galleria,* my character was Sophia Loren, and I think that the way I created her character was useful for me, for her, for all of us.

– *Was the film mostly shot in the studio?*

– One part was entirely shot in the studio, but there were also a lot of scenes filmed on location. The screenplay was very good. It was the story of a group of variety players, *"guitti,"* untalented actors – those small companies that travel around Italy, going from one town to another, trying to get a big theater run for their show. The film's title alluded to a place in Rome, the Galleria Colonna, where – just like in Naples or other cities – actors out of work and looking for contracts got together. The café in the gallery was a beautiful place because of its genuineness: aging singers, old music-hall soubrettes... During those days, the *avanspettacolo* [low-brow opening variety shows before a film, *Trans.*] still existed... It could have been a fascinating movie. Unfortunately, I didn't bring this real world to the screen; I should have treated it in a realistic way and used authentic characters from the Galleria Colonna. But instead of unknown players we had famous actors. How much better those old has-beens would have been. In the midst of these people there was one young girl, a real knock-out, whom everyone mistreated, even rejected, when in fact she alone was the one to keep the company going. This poor girl sacrificed herself continually, like a lovely object, to save the others from of all sorts of predicaments: the decadence of the group was such that only this young girl's beauty could keep it from collapsing.

– *The theme of the Galleria Colonna, a place where actors looking for work get together, was used again by Alberto Sordi in* Stardust.

– It wasn't just by chance – the author of the story for *Ci troviamo in galleria* was the same writer as *Stardust,* Ruggero Maccari.

– *The next film,* Wild Love, *was very successful.*

– *Wild Love* was my second film; in fact in some ways, it was my first. It was a film that I had chosen myself, unlike *Ci troviamo in galleria* which was a film I had been asked to make, and which already had a story – one which I had accepted for commercial reasons. In *Wild Love,* a Pasolini-type of atmosphere could already be felt a little, even if the mood of the film was perhaps gentler. I wanted to do something with Pasolini, we had only just met. At the time, he was an unknown author and they wouldn't let me use him. So Pasolini didn't collaborate on *Wild Love;* yet there are certain things in the film that suggest the coming of Pasolini, the boys, the little square... All of this was done in a way that wasn't yet Pasolinian; it was more what I would call a 'Pasolini approach.' Indeed, after the film, Pasolini published *Ragazzi di vita:* and from that moment on, there was this yearning for Pasolini. So, *Wild Love* was a film that really interested me a lot even if Pasolini wasn't involved directly at all, it's a question of inspiration only, a transition before coming to Roman dialect and certain neighborhoods of the city: my leading actors were boys from Trastevere, not yet the outskirts, the *borgate*.

– *Coming as you did from Tuscany, where you had lived for many years, when you settled in Rome didn't you get the impression that you had entered a different cultural universe?*

– Oh yes. I lived in Florence for a long time, studied in Florence... And in those days Florence was still a city that had an important cultural life. You could even say that writers obtained their consecration in Florence: the literary critics were there. A world which, in short, I later met up with again in Rome, people such as Pratolini for example. Of course, Florence and Rome were different: for me, I entered Rome's cultural world via my studies. While at the Centro Sperimentale, I continued my architectural studies. In Rome, I met a lot of young people, and then Pasolini and later others, who also collaborated with me, Moravia, Parise...

Beginnings in Italian comedy on the theme of apartment hunting: Cristina Gajoni, Peppino De Filippo, Laura Adani, Cathia Caro in Mauro Bolognini's *Arrangiatevi!*

– *Were your architectural studies also a lot of help to you as a film director?*

– Yes, they were a great help. Architecture, the way it's studied in Florence, is sort of a timeless architecture; we even had subjects that weren't offered at universities in other Italian cities; for example, decorative subjects, nude and landscape drawing... in other words, observing things, people, trees. One important exam we had to pass consisted in drawing trees, faces, bodies. This kind of careful observation is very much present in my films. So, in a some ways, my architectural studies were extremely important to me. Maybe if I had studied in another city things would have been different. In Florence – at least in the first years – our courses had practically nothing to do with reinforced concrete. It wasn't until the end of our studies that it was covered. Before that, we had a lot of this preparatory work that began from the distant past – perhaps too distant: people criticized the university of Florence for this a lot; it was considered a university from the nineteenth century. Nevertheless, in my case, it proved very useful.

– *To go back to your filmography again, after* Wild Love *you made* La vena d'oro.

– That was a film conceived for an actress who at the time was very famous in Italy, Marta Toren; she was a big star. Its theme was one that had always interested me; I took it up again in a more serious way a few years later in *Agostino,* based on Moravia's very beautiful novel: the theme of sexual discovery through a mother. In *La vena d'oro,* however, this was all treated in a very sentimental way.

– *During that time, you also made comedies such as* Guardia, guardia scelta, brigadiere e maresciallo *or* Arrangiatevi!

– First of all, as you French say, I'm all for 'bread-and-butter' work. I should also add that, frankly, I feel like running the other way when it comes to comedy. But even so, people keep offering me comedies and every time I've made one, despite my reticence, I've always succeeded, I've never been wrong about how they should be done. *Arrangiatevi!* with Totò was a huge success. The episodes that I also wrote in *La mia signora* or *The Witches,* with Silvana Mangano and Alberto Sordi, were very funny, too. I don't like comedy, and yet it's a genre that I'm very good at – maybe everyone likes what he can't do. During my life I think I've refused hundreds of comedies with the best comedians. Nevertheless, I've also worked with some very great comedy actors such as Totò or Alberto Sordi.

– *I recently saw* Arrangiatevi!; *it's a very good film.*

– When it was released, the film was not successful with the critics; they said it was an easy comedy, etcc... However, there was one critic, Pietro Bianchi, who wrote a veritable hymn to the film. Germi, too, liked it a lot. In *Arrangiatevi!,* there was quite a strong message: the desecration of the Italian family – in those days the family was untouchable. The film told the story of a family that finally ends up living in a former brothel. For this film I had extraordinary actors as well, Franca Valeri, Peppino De Filippo, Vittorio Caprioli and especially Totò. If I had liked comedy more, I think I would have been very successful at it. But this wasn't what I wanted to do. Nevertheless, I must say that I have wonderful memories of *Arrangiatevi,* thanks to the actors, who were

all so good: we really had a lot of fun during the shooting.

– *Totò was greatly neglected by the critics, and yet he was a tremendously talented actor.*

– In my film he was "essential." In a way because of my own personal taste, but also as a result of the influence of my architectural studies. I remember a famous professor who, while we were drawing architectural projects, walked between the tables and without ever looking at what we were doing, put his hand on our work and said, "Remove." Then, he came by again, "Remove." Basically, with Totò I remember having done the same thing, "Remove, remove," to finally get to the essential. In the beginning he didn't like this at all, and used to say I was taking everything away from him. But he was so rich, so extraordinary, that I would tell him, "You can remove–*you* can do it, others can't." In the film, he really does some wonderful things, everything is there, nothing is too much, nothing is not enough. I really loved Totò. Now, when I see the film, sometimes I get angry with myself: "Too bad I asked Totò to remove things, I should have told him to add even more." Totò was so great that it was a sin to ask him to take anything out. Nevertheless, as far as the character is concerned, I must admit that it was successful.

– *With* Marisa la civetta *and* Young Husbands, *you began working with Pasolini. Was it you who asked him to join as one of your collaborators?*

– Yes, it was me. In those days Pier Paolo wasn't working as a screenwriter yet. In the early years, everyone was very hostile towards my working with him, not only producers, but also friends. The dialogues in *Young Husbands* were unusual, perhaps literary, they had something special – I wouldn't even know how to describe it – in any case these dialogues were very different from the normal blah-blah. Pasolini was very different, and his dialogues had a strange sound to them. I remember that when we held the première of *Young Husbands* at Cinecittà, a lot of people came: actors, actresses, famous film directors, there was Antonioni, Fellini, and many others. Normally, in those days you invited friends, and at

A naturalist drama in turn-of-the-century Florence whose atmosphere is reconstructed with a painter's sensitivity. Romolo Valli and Jean-Paul Belmondo in Mauro Bolognini's *La Viaccia/The Love Makers*.

the end of the screening they applauded. That evening, at the end of the film no one applauded. No one even dared leave the theater because they didn't want to have to face me. No one had the courage to say anything to me, nothing; it was tragic. And me, I was standing in the back of the theater, and I had to go out so that they would finally leave. Their reaction, I think, was partly due to the unusual dialogues. Some friends took me by the arm along the lanes of the Cinecittà grounds – for example, Fellini, and said to me, "But why do you do things like that?" That night they really demoralized me. Nevertheless, I got the feeling that it was my collaboration with Pasolini that had really bothered them. So, I decided right

then and there to continue working with Pier Paolo. We made *On Any Street, Bell'Antonio, From a Roman Balcony* together.

– For On Any Street, *Pasolini wrote both the story and the screenplay, didn't he?*

– In the beginning, Pasolini – who was the only person I felt like working with – had a little one-page story; then little by little, the screenplay grew out of it.

– I find the casting in On Any Street *very interesting, particularly the choice of the actresses. Did Pasolini agree with this choice?*

The "booming" debut of princess Soraya in cinema (with Richard Harris) in Mauro Bolognini's episode "Gli amanti celebri" in the film *I tre volti*.

– Pier Paolo wasn't happy with the actors. He liked *From a Roman Balcony* more than *On Any Street.* I wanted to break out of neorealism a little; I didn't want to take boys off the street, but rather established actors, Laurent Terzieff, Jean-Claude Brialy. For me it was a sort of liberation. Pasolini didn't like this choice at all. Later, he took this back; he liked Elsa Martinelli and the other actresses a lot. At first he used to say that mine was a forced effort. He was very intelligent, though, and accepted my choices nevertheless – yet at the same time all the while saying he would have made the film differently. For example, Franco Citti was working with us on the screenplay and Pasolini told me, "As for me, I'd make the film with Citti instead of Terzieff, but if you want Terzieff, make it with Terzieff." And indeed, when he made *Accattone*, he of course used Citti. Basically, he wanted his screenplay to be filmed in a certain way. Perhaps my choice was also a way of keeping my independence; I didn't feel like making the movie with the same people who were sitting around the table with us while we were working. Many of the scenes were written in restaurants with Citti and other friends,

based, in fact, on real life. But in order to shoot the film freely, I needed to break out of the screenplay. So, when I started shooting I didn't see Pier Paolo anymore. This made him suffer a lot, but I didn't even want him on the set. Of course, we were very good friends; my attitude was not at all polemical. I told him not to come to the shooting because it would just upset him: you'll be seeing Terzieff, Elsa Martinelli when you had wanted Citti. So, there's no point in your coming." In the end, though, he was quite happy with it. Of all the films I made with him, the one he liked the best, the one he said *yes* to at the end of the screening, was *From a Roman Balcony.* Nevertheless, it was a film that filled me with great bitterness, despite Pasolini's opinion. When the time came for the film's première I didn't even want to go; I had the feeling the film would be jeered and that the evening was going to be disastrous. "No, you're crazy, it's going to be a success," Pasolini told me. He left for the Adriano with some friends, Laura Betti too, I think. As soon as the credits appeared, people started whistling loudly, even before they had seen the film – a disaster from the very start.

– Nevertheless, the film is full of good things, particularly that long shot of the interior courtyard of that lower-class building which the story begins and ends with.

– It was the first time, apart from a few modest efforts in *On Any Street,* that I had held the camera myself, a technique which since then, I've used a lot. I shot all of that courtyard sequence with a hand-held camera; it was my first time shooting such a long sequence like that. Now, I'm always with the camera. Later, Pasolini also worked in the same way.

– Most likely Pasolini was already thinking of becoming a director at the time.

– Yes, of course. It was during that period he began coming to see me edit and used to say, "But why don't you join these?" And I would answer, "Pier Paolo, you're crazy, you can't do that – a minimum of cinematic grammar does exist." And then he would be quiet... then ask me again, "But why not?" In fact, he was always right, he never a made mistake. And his suggestion, seemingly rather absurd, would have something quite natural about it. Pasolini was absolutely right. Instinctively I rebelled; but then realized that I had someone by my side who never came up with a bad idea. I took back what I had said and offered, "Let's try." And it was really good.

– In On Any Street *and* From a Roman Balcony, *the feeling of Pasolinian despair emerges very strongly.*

– I think that this feeling was something that both Pasolini and myself carried within us since birth. This was what made us feel close; it was really the cement that bound us one to the other.

– This despair lies at the very heart of Pasolini's universe.

– I believe that Pasolini managed to reach the furthest depths of his despair: a despair that, in a way, I envied him very much for.

– Your collaboration with Pasolini therefore meant something very important to you, something that went beyond work.

– Yes, for me my collaboration with Pasolini was extremely important. I miss him very much. Pasolini had urged me to make my last film, *The Inheritance.* "You must make it... you must make it," he had told me. A few days before his death, I met with him and talked about the problems I was having with the screenplay, "You must read this script, Pier Paolo, I'm really worried about it." But he had replied, "But what's there to read? Throw it all away, take Chelli's book, that's all you have to do. Everything – everything is in the book." But I insisted, "Yes, but please read the screenplay for me anyway." But after that, unfortunately... A terrible thing...

– In 1961 The Love Makers *marked a turning point perhaps in your work – not only in terms of the choice of period, place and characters, but also in the extreme attention devoted to form.*

– Actually, I think that in the previous films there was already a certain successful rendering of form. Moreover, this was something that Pasolini reproached me a lot for saying, "It's too much..." In *On Any Street* or *From a Roman Balcony*, I pretended not to hear him, since the shirts were already drying in the courtyard... Pasolini hated that sort of thing. However, to me it came naturally. I never thought about it; it just happened like that. I was holding the camera for the first time. It was a way of writing: maybe this was my architectural background coming back. And so I told him, "I never think about it." I never wasted a minute composing a shot.

– Perhaps this involuntary sensitivity to form is something innate.

– No doubt. Remember, *The Love Makers* was shot very quickly; Belmondo in fact only stayed in Florence for four weeks. We shot half the film without him: he had to leave, so we worked with his double. The entire film was made like that. Of course, the movie had been carefully prepared beforehand. And then, I had Florence there in front of me. It was my first time shooting in Florence, where I had studied, the streets, the squares, the buildings that I had drawn – everything came back to me. And then there was Pratolini's contribution to the screenplay; his dialogues were very literary – let's just say that it wasn't a text that could ever have belonged to neorealism. His words called for a particular music, nothing haphazard, I had to find just the right match. Generally, I think that my search for what we might call "form" is never an end in itself; I always look for life in all things, and then, if I find it, it's unconscious. When I shoot in Florence or in Rome, I'm always looking for life in the streets, in the costumes. Form comes after that; I don't look first for form in order to find life. Now, that's something I'm often accused of. I'm perfectly honest with myself in this, I know, because I never indulge in the study of form for its own sake, though it may sometimes seem so. I look first for truth, for life; my presumption is to find life in things. And so, I can't stand being criticized for certain things: for example, that my costumes sometimes seem too studied, such as in *The Love Makers*. Even Piero Tosi was accused of this. Nothing more untrue could be said – Tosi worked hard to find the truth in costumes, by rummaging in farmers' wardrobes and getting all sorts of clothes from places like that. This was to avoid creating the kind of film costumes that so please the critics but which I find so disgusting; they so represent cinematic fiction. So, this was what I was really looking for, my objective. Of course, this means extremely painstaking work, very meticulous. We even thought about the dust to cover people with, if possible. Anyway, after this, when I begin shooting – I usually make films very quickly – I don't have time to stop and look for a beautiful shot. I film, unleashing people into a street and then, with camera in hand, go out there. Of course, I want everything that's in view to be right; but after that, I just let everything be born, everything that has to happen must happen. So, for me, the preparation is definitely done with extreme care. I'm not meticulous about it, I'm *neurotic* when it comes to preparation. When I know that everything is right, this makes me feel free. I don't intentionally look for beautiful images, pretty shots, never.

– *Many of your films were set during the end of the nineteenth century or early twentieth century. Was this a deliberate choice?*

– Yes and no. Certainly the themes of that period, even in terms of social problems, were more or less the same as today's – those were problems it was easy to bring up-to-date. Moreover, quite honestly, everything our literature is made up of today can be traced back to that era and even, perhaps, to the period before that. And then, choosing to bring the past to the screen doesn't mean that I don't want to make films about the present, even perhaps tomorrow. And I would even like to do a more remote past. But the more we go back in time, the more complicated it becomes – difficult from all points of view, including production. I'd be very happy to make a film about the Medici, Machiavelli, though it's impossible to take on Machiavelli's epoch without complications, whereas I *can* handle Florence at the end of the last century, simply by getting rid of the traces of the present from the locations where I film. If I want to make a movie about a more distant past, I also need to have greater production possibilities at my disposal, which are inexistent in Italy.

– *The fact that your films are all shot in real settings gives them their beauty.*

– Basically, the films I make are very low-budget – almost improvised movies. I work as if I were making films set in modern times. I shot *The Love Makers* just like I did *On Any Street*. Instead of having the costumes of prostitutes on the streets today, we had the prostitutes in brothels. To me, the attitude is the same, the work is the same. *Metello* and my other films were made like this, too.

– *Your films take a new look at a number of cities: Florence, Rome, Bologna, Venice, Milan, Turin, Padua, Catania, Trieste...*

– I wanted very much to do this. Perhaps I was most successful in *Careless* with Trieste. This was difficult, since the city of the twenties had somewhat disappeared. The inhabitants of Trieste rediscovered their city in the film and I think it made them very happy.

– *What gave you the idea of adapting* Careless *to the screen, that masterpiece of twentieth-century*

Italian literature, when initially it seemed so hard to make into a film?

– First of all, because Svevo's novel was one of my favorites. Of all the films I've made, it's the only one I'd like to remake, not because I'm not happy with it, but because I think it can be remade hundreds of times. I'd like to keep redoing *Careless* all my life, a bit like a painter who keeps painting the same landscape, the same bottle. When I started preparing *Careless,* I had just finished *The Love Makers* with Pratolini. Pratolini kept on saying to me, "Don't make it, you shouldn't even touch it, leave that book alone." Anyway, he really discouraged me. At the time I had just started working on *Metello.* And then, the project was shelved, I wasn't

going to make the film for eight years, and I decided to make *Careless.* I said to Pratolini, "Since we're going to make *Metello* together, whatever you do, don't go to see *Careless,* because you won't like it." One day I received a letter from Pratolini saying he was in Florence. One evening, while walking down the street in the howling wind, he had seen *Careless* billed in a theater. This was two or three years after the film's release. In his letter, Pratolini told me that he had gone inside to see it, and that he had found it very beautiful: "You won." I was filled with joy at this, since it had come from Pratolini, from someone who had been against making the film. Svevo's book is exceptional and I think the movie has some good things in it: the city, the characterization of the hero's sister, and even, I

A beauty who, by exposing herself somewhat, provoked a scandal (with a complaint of obscenity lodged against the film). Gina Lollobrigida in the episode by Mauro Bolognini, "Monsignor Cupido," in the film *Le bambole/The Dolls.*

think, the character portrayed by Claudia Cardinale. The only character who gave rise to some reservations was the hero played by Anthony Franciosa. This wasn't because his acting wasn't as good as the others, but perhaps he just wasn't convincing in that particular role. I wanted him to play this character and was happy with his performance. Franciosa was very much like the character in the book; he resembled him: it wasn't necessary to have a man who was physically old, we needed a young man, since senility is interior. Visually, Franciosa was strong, and therefore the image had to go beyond this apparent force. It was complicated for Franciosa to portray the twisted, neurotic sensitivity of the character. Really, I don't know; I'd like to see the film again and see how I feel.

– *Svevo's book was published for the first time in 1898 though your film is set in the twenties. Can you explain this change of period?*

– There weren't any particular reasons for deciding to do this, but rather a *reasoning*. The book was written at the end of the nineteenth century though the final edition, very different from that of 1898, was dated 1927. Success did not come overnight. Svevo only began to be recognized in the twenties. Therefore, in a way, that's the reason why my screenwriters, Tullio Pinelli and Goffredo Parise, and I decided to set the film in that period. Also, it was easier to reconstruct the city for the shooting: recreating nineteenth-century Trieste would have been very difficult. We chose the twenties both due to the technical problem of the sets, and a literary concern, so that the film's period would coincide with the time the book became a success. At any rate, the problem was relatively unimportant since the main character's behavior wasn't affected. Even a modern adaptation could be made.

– *After* Careless, *you made* Agostino. *How did you adapt Moravia's novel?*

– I didn't change much in the book to make the film. I wrote the screenplay with Parise. Moravia had authorized us to change whatever we wanted to. In fact, though, we didn't make any major changes. I set the movie in a different city than the

one in the novel: I preferred Venice to Viareggio because I wanted more water. The theme of water was also present in Viareggio, a maritime city, but in Venice it was even more so. In Venice, the theme was gentler than a city directly on the sea. *Agostino* was one of the films I most liked making; I think it was quite a strong film when I made it. And then, its theme was very beautiful.

– *The film wasn't very successful was it?*

– For some reason the film was billed for a week and then was removed and disappeared forever. The only reason *Agostino* was released in Stockholm was because Ingrid Thulin owned the film for Sweden and she had a percentage on the distribution. The film wasn't distributed anywhere else, it was shelved – mysterious reasons...

– *During the sixties, a period that was not always a good one for Italian cinema, you collaborated on an entire series of episode films.*

– Yes, that period of episode films made one after another... Of all the episodes I shot during those years, there's only one I really like: the first one. This was an episode that at first was shot for a film to be called *Il grand Guignol* and then was taken out and included with other episodes in *La donna è una cosa meravigliosa*. My episode was called *La balena bianca*; it was a story that took place in a circus, with midgets and a cannonball woman called "the white whale." I worked very hard on this film, taken from a screenplay Parise and I had written. Venice invited us to show the episode, out of competition, at the final evening of the Festival. It was a disaster; I was insulted, the two midgets fled afraid the public was going to lynch them. I was told the film was a mass of vulgarities and other things like that; and yet I truly believe it's the best thing I've ever done.

– *During that time you also made two feature films,* Madamigella di Maupin *and* Arabella.

– *Madamigella di Maupin* was really unfortunate since the book by Théophile Gautier, *Mademoiselle de Maupin*, was very beautiful and I liked it a lot. But sometimes that great machine which a film is, goes out of control and there's no steering it any-

In nineteenth-century Paris, reconstructed in Italy, a pathetic story of a prostitute and a pimp. Ottavia Piccolo and Antonio Falsi in Mauro Bolognini's *Bubù*.

more. There were a series of mishaps during this film. It was supposed to be a German production with lots of money, and then everything fell through. We ran aground in Yugoslavia. It was the only "adventure" film I ever made. All the others, even with low budgets, in Italy or abroad, were made within well-defined structures. This was really an adventure. We went in blindfolded and the film turned out the way it did.

Arabella was an English-style comedy made with Virna Lisi who, at that time, was very popular. Lisi arrived from the States and the film was shot in English with James Fox, who was also a very famous actor then (riding high on his success in Losey's *The Servant*); the elderly English actress Margaret Rutherford, and Terry Thomas, a comedy film star. Tackling comedy English-style didn't really appeal to me – comedy is already hard enough in Italian; in a foreign language it was really difficult. There were some things that turned

out well; for example, Giancarlo Giannini in his comic role played English-style. Giannini, in those days, was more or less still a budding actor.

– From 1969 with That Splendid November *you returned to more major undertakings.*

– I hate *That Splendid November;* what's more I didn't get along very well with Gina Lollobrigida. In the film there were some good things: the Sicilian backdrop, the family. But I think the necessary element of courage was missing here in the study of the amorous relationship between the aunt and the nephew. In the end it's always the director's fault: in this film, what's really missing is a high point, not that you have to have a memorable scene in every film. But in *That Splendid November*, it was important to build up to a high point, which I never found, that escaped me. So I don't consider it an important film.

– *I find* L'assoluto naturale *a very original film.*

– I've worked with Parise many times. He's someone I greatly esteem and whom I consider still today one of the commanding voices in Italy, an intelligent voice. So, we started with a text, not really a comedy, but rather notes for a comedy. It was sort of a challenge – something that wasn't to be done – to make a film out of it. In this case, I liked the idea of trying to do something that normally couldn't be done, shouldn't be done. The film seemed liked it had an intelligent and funny text to go by. So, it was more an intellectual rather than a popular choice: in general, I must admit honestly, I like making popular films. Nevertheless, I wanted to try making this film – cinema can also give you the chance to do things like that: cold, intellectual, in a

way, simplified. It was, you can call it, a test: but Italy isn't a country where you can conduct this type of experiment and so the film didn't do very well. Whatever the case may be, I was happy with the film; it's one I like.

– Metello *brings us to one of your most famous films. Do you also consider it to be one of your most important?*

– That's difficult to say. Certainly, the fact that I made *Metello* is important to me; it's one of the films, with *Careless,* that means the most to me. It was a film I had prepared long before, and prepared like no other film. Lila Lenopri had drawn all the models, the costumes, and the hero was supposed to be Albert Finney who, at the time, had just made

Rome at the end of the last century, recreated with exceptional subtlety to portray the rifts in a family over an inheritance. Anthony Quinn and Dominique Sanda in Mauro Bolognini's *L'eredità Ferramonti/The Inheritance.*

Saturday Night and Sunday Morning but hadn't made *Tom Jones* yet. And then, the film was cancelled. So, after all that preparation everything was stopped and the film was shelved for eight or nine years. I was finally only able to make it after accepting to work on a shoestring budget and with very few actors: Massimo Ranieri and Ottavia Piccolo weren't famous yet; as for Lucia Bosè, she returned to the screen as a friend, not as an actress. The whole film was made with friends.

– *The lack of means doesn't show in the film.*

– Nevertheless the film was made under those conditions. The film meant a lot to me; it still does now and I wanted to go ahead and shoot it even under those difficult circumstances. One part of the film is among the best things I've ever done, I think; not everything one hundred percent, but for example, the characters played by Ottavio Piccolo, Lucia Bosè, and also in part by Massimo Ranieri, were successful. It was severely criticized that the film was sentimental and not political enough. But I like it *because* it's sentimental: I'm not ashamed to use feelings, and if a film moves people, all the better. However, I'm accused of moving people; I must not move, I must show political problems. But I'm not a politician; the story I told interested me first of all as an expression of the human condition, and then as a political reflection. It's the character's condition that interested me, and this didn't become political except as a result. And anyway, I don't believe in politics when it's made up of all the dogmas of the "political." I can't make films like a politician, I make them as a director. I think Picasso said something very true: "A well-painted rose is more political, has more political value, than a badly written manifesto."

– *Films that are much more markedly political are possible, but it is indisputable that your approach to filmmaking is perfectly coherent.*

– It's a choice, a declared choice; there's no ambiguity.

– *After* Metello, *you made another film in somewhat the same vein,* Bubù.

– That film was a real heartbreak for me. I loved Charles-Louis Philippe's book, upon which *Bubù* [1] was greatly based. It was a film I wanted very much to make and I worked very hard on it, really very diligently. I don't understand why *Bubù* was never released in France when they distribute so many films there [2]. *Bubù* would have appealed to the French, if only for the novel: I talked to some French friends, they weren't even familiar with the book by Charles-Louis Philippe, though in Italy this text left its mark on an entire kind of literature; it gave birth to many other things. Moreover, at the time, Ottavia Piccolo had been awarded a prize at Cannes; so a known actress was in it who could have helped if the film had been released in France.

– *Where was the film shot?*

– In Milan and Turin, and then I created a sort of collage to suggest an industrial city in the North. Maybe that was my first mistake: I should have shot the film in Paris as in the novel. That was a weakness on my part, but on the other hand, filming in Paris would have posed a lot of problems. And then, the public no doubt didn't like the fact that the characters were so young. I carefully noted a letter that Philippe had written to a friend concerning the illustrations of his book: "Today I saw the drawings for the illustrations of the cover and pages of *Bubù*. I feel very sad because I see that the heroine was made to look like a real prostitute and the hero like a pimp, completely conventional. Instead, I wanted the heroine to be a young girl who worked as a seamstress and he, a baker who stays a baker; they are young people, young people just like any others."

I think that this mistake kept the book from being fully understood. For my part, in the film I should have perhaps made them look even younger: the book's wonderful insight was that he was in fact a worker, a baker, and she a seamstress; they become a prostitute and a pimp, but nevertheless never lose their qualities as young people. No doubt I should have emphasized this more at the beginning of the film by giving more details about the

---

[1] *Bubu de Montparnasse,* Paris 1901.

[2] The film was finally released in France in March 1977.

two characters' origins, their homes, their jobs, their milieu. Instead, the public just thought that Ottavia Piccolo didn't look enough like a prostitute, and Antonio Falsi, not enough like a pimp. The theme of syphilis wasn't bound to be particularly appealing to people either. In the end, the film was rejected by both public and critics. Naturally, I personally like the film very much.

– In the midst of several costume films, Imputazione di omicidio per uno studente *made you return to a movie set in our own times.*

– That film was somewhat a "work accident." First of all, there was this beautiful story developed out of an outline by Ugo Pirro. Pirro had written this outline several years before, even before making *Investigation of a Citizen Above Suspicion* with Elio Petri, and it had been handed around to a number of producers and film directors. The story had the indisputable force of a burning issue: these kinds of themes must be treated right away. So, I made the film – and then perhaps this type of story is not really me – the subject had become dated, which was a serious handicap for a story so bound to 'news in brief' columns of a certain time. The film, I think, was made five years after the story was written. It was a very simple story: during a confrontation between police and students, a policeman and a student are killed. The inquest apparently only seeks to discover the policeman's murderer, whereas the student's murderer is not sought. The magistrate in charge of the inquest finds himself in a dramatic situation: his own son, a student, confesses to his father that it was he who killed the policeman but says that he won't give proof of the murder nor confess to the police unless the magistrate succeeds in discovering who killed the student. The subject was very beautiful but the film was released right at the time when a whole series of films on police and students were being shown... Also, the film had a better title in the beginning, *Se muore un poliziotto;* but they didn't keep that title.

– Libera amore mio! *was shot in 1973 and wasn't distributed until 1975. Why was it delayed?*

– Libera amore mio! was a very important film to me, one in which Claudia Cardinale also gave a great performance. Unfortunately, it was a film that was shelved for two years at Italnoleggio because of production problems. When it was released, its significance had changed and it was not at all successful. Indeed, the film, that should have been prophetic, had become polemical. The movie ended with a prophecy that in fact later came true; that is, with the idea that the Fascists would reorganize and be responsible for bombings. By the time the film was distributed, the Fascists had already set off these bombs and everyone knew it; whereas when I had made the film, the bombings hadn't happened yet and no one was aware – at least not officially, not the general public – that they were reorganizing. Therefore, the relationship between the film and the context of the time had completely changed. *Libera amore mio!* was severely boycotted and greatly mistreated. It was, nevertheless, a film that made me very happy because it appealed to the people to whom I was close, people I'm still close to. For example, after seeing the film, Visconti sent me an enthusiastic telegram.

– The film was based on a true story, wasn't it?

– Yes, it was a story by Luciano Vincenzoni, a subject based upon, with a few changes, the story of Vincenzoni's mother. *Libera amore mio!* is a film about the resistance during the Fascist era, the story of a female anarchist. The film begins like a grotesque comedy, a little like Fascism itself in its early years, and then, little by little, transforms into tragedy.

– And this brings us to your most recent films, Drama of the Rich, Down the Ancient Staircase, The Inheritance.

– Drama of the Rich *was an Italian front-page item, the Murri Case, a story heavy with a thousand meanings. In any country, if a similar case had exploded, writers would definitely have written novels based on it. It was a fascinating story which I brought to the screen with great enthusiasm. In some ways, it was an easy film to make, a good screenplay, actors I liked...

Mauro Bolognini: *La villa del venerdì* **with Joanna Pacula and Julian Sands.**

Down the Ancient Staircase wasn't received well; however, for me it was an intense experience, a film I liked a lot. Madness is something that at first makes people flee. The first time I set foot in an insane asylum I felt like giving up doing the film and then, little by little, that world began to fascinate me and I wanted to tell this story, I wanted the public to get to know what insanity was, without the repulsion that, of course, we naturally feel at first – when you enter an asylum, madness so deforms everything that your first instinct is to run away – but rather with an attitude of understanding. It's not easy to spend the whole day with a mentally ill person; I don't mean those who are quiet, but rather the ones locked up, those who are deformed. You can't imagine what being in contact with such tragic beings is like: it's very hard. And then, little by little, day after day, you start realizing that it's possible to meet someone's glance, to find a moment of contact. And that instant is so great that you want to stay. However, the first reaction is to run away, to reject madness. I therefore didn't want to make a film that

the public would immediately reject. I wanted to make it less harsh and get beyond the first contact with madness, that contact that is so tragic. Maybe deciding to do this was a mistake, as was also, no doubt, wanting to make a film more about madness than about insane asylums. In those days, it would probably have been better to look at the problem of psychiatric hospitals; as for me, however, I was more interested in the mystery of insanity: why do we go mad? Why, one day out of the blue, does insanity suddenly appear? Usually, 90 times out of 100, some say 99 out of 100, madness can be explained by social causes. Nevertheless, there is still that one time when there aren't any social justifications: it's not because a person was forced to live in a single room with ten other people, or in the bleakest poverty, that he goes mad. Of course, in most cases, insanity clearly does have social roots. However, the problem of insanity would be solved if its causes were only of this nature. But this isn't the case. This experience made me very sad. I participated in a tragic debate, so tragic it would have made you want to

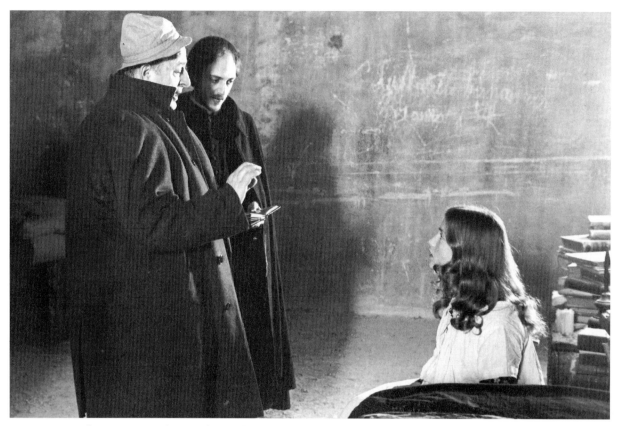

Not missing a thing, Mauro Bolognini during the shooting of *La storia vera della Signora delle camelie/The True Story of Camille* with Isabelle Huppert and Fabio Traversa.

leave, during which everyone only spoke in political terms: "Madness is simple; we knock down walls, we find solutions to family problems and the problem of madness is solved." This isn't true: a woman living in poverty, beaten by her husband, doesn't go mad. But then, another woman in the same conditions – husband, children, poverty – does go insane. So, what I mean is, there isn't such a simple link between madness and social factors. There are some cases that are a true mystery, and this was what interested me.

I didn't see Bellocchio's film, *Matti da slegare.* I know it was a very beautiful film. I couldn't see it, a little out of laziness; it was my own fault really because I like Bellocchio a lot, and then, a bit because I was afraid to see it and wanted to make my own film without having seen Bellocchio's. Nevertheless, I know what it's about, I know it's a wonderful film, poetic, shot with the patients of an asylum. I know what this means, having been in one.

However, I wasn't conducting an investigation, I was bringing a novel to the screen. And therefore I was involved in a different process, not poetic or political or tragic reporting; I was telling a slightly romanticized story, with thirties costumes, with more emphasis on madness, on certain characters, than on asylums: this choice somewhat shifted the film's central theme; *Down the Ancient Staircase* seemed to be a film that wanted to avoid the problem of the asylum, a problem that I myself didn't want to avoid completely. The tragic thing nowadays is that anyone who doesn't choose to go the same way as the majority is rejected and his work disdained. The two paths both exist: I would have loved to have undertaken what Bellocchio did, having also had some experience of psychiatric asylums. Certainly, I would not have done it as well as he did; nevertheless, it is something that I would have liked to have done: sometimes in the asylum, I filmed the patients. But in my film, I couldn't use them, I didn't get permission. Oh, if I could only have stolen one of those patients' looks just once with my camera... Instead, I had false nurses, false patients; it was very hard to find the same faces already glimpsed, rebuild something that wasn't real. I think that you can recreate anything except madness; madness cannot be copied. Madness can be light; there isn't just spectacular madness. There are the insane who don't do a thing; they are nothing but vibrations, imperceptible. An actor can't express that, he always has to overplay madness, pretend, compose. So, these were the limitations within which I was forced to make my film. Perhaps my choice wasn't right; nevertheless, I had to take a certain direction...

– *Where did you shoot the film?*

– The exteriors were shot in the San Salvi asylum in Florence. Nevertheless, the insane you see are extras who came to Florence everyday. In the whole film, there are only two real characters, two nurses, who had been there for twenty years, thirty years, two ex-patients who still live in the asylum as nurses. So, in the film there isn't one real patient. The interiors were shot in Rome, in the abandoned building of the Istituto San Michele, a former reformatory.

– *What do you think of Marcello Mastroianni as the doctor?*

– Choosing Mastroianni was in my opinion a good choice. He was an Italian doctor, a doctor from Lucca, from the Italian provinces. He wasn't Max Von Sydow. In Lucca, there aren't any Max Von Sydows. Of course, for an international public, Von Sydow was very good: the doctor with the steel eyes, eyes of ice. However, in Lucca, the doctor who lives there, this doctor described by Mario Tobino in his novel, is someone like Mastroianni, an Italian, bound to our soil, our landscape. Around Lucca there aren't any glaciers. I think Mastroianni understood this provincialism very well, the smallness of the character, his disorder. I liked the character that way, with his Tuscan madness, with his ties, with a certain authenticity in the places and the period. Naturally, from a more spectacular point

of view, I could have chosen an actor à la Bergman. But I was making a film set in Lucca in 1930.

– *Before becoming a film,* The Inheritance *was first of all a book, a novel by Gaetano Carlo Chelli published in 1883.*

– It was Pasolini who, in a way, rediscovered Chelli by publishing a review on *The Inheritance* – the book, not the film of course. Pasolini exalted it, saying that it was one of the most beautiful books in Italian literature. Of course, he exaggerated in order to be heard; he always went to extremes to make people listen. In any case, Chelli's book is without a doubt a good book, one of those rare books in our literature that describes the Roman petty-bourgeois world. And so, what interested me was its description of a family's destruction and also one of the characters – the antagonist – that is, the character of the brother-in-law, the politician. This was a "good" man, an "honest" man, who stayed home; who plotted everything from home, while his wife was apparently the monster, though she was no more monstrous than the man. In fact, she was a woman who had received a certain kind of upbringing and who advanced in the pursuit of money like a saint – she was bent on attaining sainthood, she was blind to everything but the conquest of money; her pursuit of evil was absolutely unbending. On the other hand, the other, the "good" man, the one to become the future politician, hatches his plot and ends up by taking all. This man, who emerges the victor, is to me the real monster, the one who gets all the money: he dreams of politics, he will be the future Italian politician.

– *You also successfully resolved the problem of the exteriors shot in the streets of Rome.*

– It was very difficult to do, a little like Trieste for *Careless.* Here, not so much because the decors were no longer existent – in Rome, the decors of the end of the last century are still very much present – but because it was difficult to isolate them from traces of the contemporary: you can't stop traffic, get rid of signs, neons, cafés, white lines on the ground. You can't invade a city with extras, actors, carriages; its unthinkable. And because of this, I had to "steal" a lot of these things and was very lucky. I shot on Via del Corso without a permit: I prepared everything on a little side street; with my assistants we stopped the buses and then the extras went down Via del Corso and I shot the scene in just one take. The *carabinieri*, the police, arrived and made us stop filming and leave. Anyway, I had already shot the scene I needed. You can do this once, but not twice. So after that, they kept an eye on us; and another time, I was just about to start shooting, it was evening with the last rays of a sunset, and the police arrived, stopped everything and made us leave. Just because of one minute, I couldn't shoot; all I needed was one minute more. The whole film was made like that. You can't work like that.

– In closing, some more general problems. First of all, I wanted to ask you if there was any particular reason why you have often adapted literary texts to the screen?

– First of all I should say – and this might not be very nice towards screenwriters in Italy, but it's the truth – that I was spoiled in the early years of my career by extraordinary collaborations. For four or five years I worked with Pasolini, you can imagine what it meant to have Pasolini as a collaborator. And then I worked with Parise who, in those days, wanted to work in cinema, but afterwards did so rather half-heartedly, and then finally gave it up. I also worked with Pratolini on the screenplay of *The Love Makers,* and later adapted his novel *Metello.* So, it's not easy to replace people like that. I really have to work with a writer, not with a professional screenwriter. When that's not possible, I prefer to first look in the library for a text that can be turned into a script by a screenwriter, a writer who writes cinema. In Italy, unfortunately, many writers often don't write for cinema, and many screenwriters *only* write for cinema. This specialization worries me. As soon as I get the feeling that someone is specialized, I block. Of course, it has happened that I've collaborated with professional screenwriters; you can't discover a new screenwriter everyday. I met a young screenwriter a while ago with whom I got along with very well. His name is Sergio Bazzini, whom I made *Drama of the Rich* and *The Inheritance* with. Bazzini is also a director. In a way, he's not really a screenwriter, he's an author – there's nothing of the professional screenwriter about him. He's a tremendously talented person; has just made *Marcia trionfale* with Marco Bellocchio; he even made a film all by himself. In short, I'm afraid of professional screenwriters.

– A book that has come before a film is a bit like a guarantee, like a fulcrum.

– Yes, that's true. Yet, at the same time, I should add that I don't distinguish between one screenplay or another in terms of where they've been drawn from. Each one of us can take stories from wherever he likes and make them his own: at the library, in the newspaper, from his own life, his autobiography. Not all my films come from novels. *Drama of the Rich* was a "news in brief" item, just as the film I'm working on now. *The Inheritance* comes from literature, but Chelli was a journalist who wrote like a columnist despite being a great writer. And then, there are some films which I really don't know where they came from.

– To go on to another characteristic of your work, the attention you devote to form isn't a search for beauty for its own sake?

– No, that's not really the case. In my defense – I dislike even saying this – I believe that it would be the most serious failure, the greatest failure, if I thought of form only for its own sake. In fact, I never think about it.

– Nevertheless, you obtain figurative results of exceptional quality. I suppose you demand a lot of your collaborators, particularly your cameramen.

– Of course. My collaborators being, of course, the set designer, the costume designer, the cameramen; these are my real collaborators – with the text, of course. I work very closely with the cameramen during all the filming: light is part of a story.

– Of course a story's meaning is also bound to the light.

Sixteenth-century Venice captured in the splendor of its urban decor and costumes. Monica Guerritore *(right)* in Mauro Bolognini's *La Venexiana*.

– So, I can't ignore the light, I can't blindfold myself; why shouldn't I look? I do look. I believe in what I'm saying, but I believe in the image, too. It's not that I think about it, but I know it's important: cinema is also image.

– *With which cameramen have you felt most at ease?*

– The two cameramen whom I felt the most at ease with were Armando Nannuzzi and Ennio Guarnieri. Nannuzzi has now become a director himself; as a cameraman, he did the most incredible things; for example, I think that in Visconti's *Ludwig* he created photography that was practically inimitable.

– *Nannuzzi is just as comfortable working in black and white as in color, isn't he?*

– Yes, that's true. I made all my early films, *On Any Street, Bell'Antonio, From a Roman Balcony, Careless,* with Nannuzzi, and also *That Splendid November* that has very beautiful color photography. In those days, the cameraman deserved even more credit, since that type of film was difficult to use. Color film has improved greatly over the past four or five years in Italy. In the United States, good film has been available for a long time, but here, until the more recent years, we had great problems printing. *That Splendid November* was therefore among the most successful films of that period in terms of photography.

– *How did you handle the transition from black and white to color?*

– Actually I made my debut with a film in color. *Ci troviamo in galleria* was a color film, one of the first Italian films in color. Even the films I shot in black and white, for example *The Love Makers,* were prepared as color films. *The Love Makers* was conceived as a film in color and was only shot in black and white because of lack of confidence in the color film available at the time, and also because of cost. Above all, no one trusted the printing facilities. At first, people didn't like color. At any rate, for me black and white is the same as color, there's no difference.

– *The only difference, perhaps, is that black and white is more abstract, more symbolic, whereas color is more realistic. In any case, your way of using color is comparable to results obtained in black and white cinema.*

– For me, what matters most is the climate, the atmosphere. So, it's not true that my films are based upon painters, even if I am constantly bombarded with comparisons to the painters whose works I've supposedly tried to recreate on the screen. Again, just recently, a very important art critic told me – he had asked to be introduced while I was in a restaurant – that he had liked *The Inheritance* and added: "We see that you've studied a German painter who painted Rome at the end of the last century." Even to this day I still don't know the name of that painter. I don't know his paintings – very secret works, very refined. Yet, this critic saw things in my film that seemed to come right out of the works of that painter. It is true that a Roman light does exist; I filmed it just the way it was, I can't invent a particular light. Certainly that gentleman who painted Rome during that period saw the same things I did, with the same light.

– *People refer to the influence of the "Macchiaioli." in* Metello.

– It's true that I've seen the "Macchiaioli" constantly, ever since I was born. I lived in Florence, studied in Florence. These are the painters who are part of me, who, I would say, are part of everyday life. I can't even really say what their influence is on me. The "Macchiaioli" depicted ordinary life in their paintings; the paintings on the walls I used to see all represented things in my house or in the houses of others, or in the streets, or in hospitals.

– *So when you're shooting, it never happens that you try to reproduce a painting.*

– No, I would be ashamed. Sometimes when you're getting documentation for a set, an interior, for example, an unusual interior that doesn't exist in real life – a dispensary, a cell, a hospital room, a dormitory – it's true that paintings can sometimes help. For costumes, I never consult fashion engravings. You sometimes come across these engravings a lot, but I don't even look at them, I always prefer to do my research using paintings – even when it would be easier to use the fashion engravings. There were painters who described an epoque very realistically, for example, who did portraits of women. I find this type of document much more interesting because it is true, whereas fashion engravings never are. The same goes for interiors: paintings are more accurate. Of course, if there's a photo, that's even better. For example, I kept the documentation I had gathered while preparing *Metello:* here is a book of photographs, of workers, masons. Even the portraits on tombstones are useful for the hairstyles. All of this is just for a start, and then after that...

Luigi Comencini

(FIRST INTERVIEW)

From Pain to Irony

– In your work we see dramas and comedies and films that are a combination of the two.

– I don't think that there are any true dramas in what I've done: drama is a rigorous genre that leaves no place for humor. However, in my films there is always humor – a certain ironic way of seeing things. Even in *Delitto d'amore,* the way the young girl acts still brings a smile, even if the episodes are very dramatic. Anyway, that's how I see it at least. I've never made any dramas in a literal sense. It seems to me that my films are characterized by pain and melancholy, mixed with irony.

– Considering the two films Bread, Love and... *there's a difference between the first and second.*

In the second film, a feeling of despair emerges that wasn't present in the first.

– What happened with these two films was very complex. I wrote the screenplay for *Bread, Love and Dreams* with Ettore Margadonna and was thinking of giving the lead to Gino Cervi. This would have given the film a certain significance: I wanted to make a rural comedy constructed with all the elegance of a comedy by Beaumarchais. This comedy was to have a very definite theme: authority's total indifference – in this case, the *carabinieri* marshall's – towards the sufferings of the people. The marshall had two sole interests in life: food and women. So, I had thought of Gino Cervi for this role and had discussed it with him. And then, for many reasons, it wasn't possible. With De Sica's intervention the problem with production was resolved and work on the film began immediately. You see, in Italy there is a reverential respect to-

Luigi Comencini,
all the passion
of a filmmaker who uses
comedy to depict
the foibles of Italian
society.

A well-intentioned priest (Adolfo Celi) coming to the rescue of the Neapolitan *scugnizzi*. Luigi Comencini's *Proibito rubare.*

wards the *carabinieri*, so much so that – I don't know why – if there were going to be a *carabinieri* marshall in the movie, you had to have an actor who would give enough weight to the role: Cervi couldn't, but with De Sica everything was considered fine...

The first day I was shooting with De Sica – I was still quite young and had only made four films – I told him, "But I see the character differently, more unpleasant, but also more true to life." De Sica said to me – I'll always remember his reply – "Well I can only play it like this, or I can't do it at all." De Sica gave a lighter more caricaturable tone to the role that helped make the film popular but which somewhat altered what I had intended. Nevertheless, I hold nothing against De Sica and

even owe him much: I learned a lot by making that film with him.

I was absolutely against making the second one. Then, one day, just joking, Margadonna and I started imagining a sequel that took up from the first film, not twenty years later, but the next day! However, we decided not to do anything with the idea. It was then that the producer Goffredo Lombardo – overjoyed with the financial success of the first film – took advantage of a slip I made in a conversation – I said, *"Bread, Love and Jealousy"* instead of *"Bread, Love and Dreams"* – and declared, "Now there's the sequel to the film!" This is a true story. Afterwards, as usual, I was weak and gave in; I would have preferred not to have made that film, even if you say that you find the second one better than the first.

– The screenplay of Bread, Love and Jealousy *was also credited to Eduardo De Filippo. To what extent did the Neapolitan author contribute to it?*

– The screenplay was written by Margadonna and myself, like the first one. De Filippo didn't do anything, with all the respect I feel for this great actor, he's a man I greatly esteem. I think it was Lombardo who imposed Eduardo De Filippo's name for production reasons: he had a contract with De Filippo.

– Is your tendency to make films that are halfway between comedy and drama a way of reaching the public?

– Yes, since I don't have a group of select admirers, intellectuals whom it would be in my interest to satisfy. My only satisfaction is success, not because I get money out of it, but because cinema is feeling – at least this is what I personally believe – since it allows me to make contact with the public. There are films I like seeing over again, hidden among the spectators, because I feel they really grip the public. I don't like seeing some of my other films when it seems the public isn't truly taken up in them. My entire career has been marked by these moments when I lose contact with the public. For example, when *La finestra sul Luna Park* – a film I like a lot, very personal, very faithful to my favorite themes – was a failure, this completely cut me off from the public. And so I told myself that I had to re-establish that contact. Since I knew how to get people to smile and laugh, I decided to make some comedies; this decision was also influenced by the phase Italian moviemaking was going through at the time – the darkest years in the history of our cinema. The year I shot *Mariti in città* I remember driving through Naples and saw billed on a poster at the Palmes, a first-run theater in the heart of town: "Today, no film. Broadcast of 'It's Double or Quits' and the San Remo Festival." Television was becoming popular in Italy though there still weren't many sets around. And movie theaters had decided to show television programs on the big screen: people went to the cinema to watch TV. That evening, they were showing "It's Double or Quits." It truly seemed like the end of cinema...

Even now, I still keep up a kind of game going with the public where I try to capture them with my films: it doesn't always work since I don't want to spoon-feed anyone. Nevertheless, I really feel that making a film that isn't successful is like building a house in which no one lives, because people don't feel good in it.

However, Italian cinema hasn't always been concerned with reaching the public. The film made out of ambition, that seeks the approval of a handful of friends, is a phenomenon that also exists in Italy. One of the worst services Italian and foreign critics have rendered to post-war Italian cinema is to have always praised those films aimed at a small audience, and to have instinctively refused successful films as being commercial: it seems absurd that a commercial film should be considered harmful. A film is good or bad. And when a quality film is popular, we should be happy and applaud.

– Referring to Delitto d'amore, *you wrote: "A film should awaken feelings and not be an exposé of ideas, since ideas come after feelings and not vice-versa."*

– Exactly. I don't believe that any openly militant film has ever changed the ideas of one single spectator. I do feel, however, that a certain kind of film puts the spectator in a mood that maybe – and I say, *maybe* – makes him see things from a slightly different angle, so that he might be more sensitive to problems that otherwise he might have been oblivious to. This, I think, is the most we can hope for; the rest is nothing but stupidity. Which was what made me like *Everybody Go Home!* so much: I had testimonies from people who at the time were still obstinately bound to Fascism but who told me after seeing the film, "We realize now that we were wrong."

This kind of comment is a tremendous satisfaction for an author. During the shooting of *Incompreso* in Florence, I remember the owner of the villa we had rented for the filming coming up to me and saying, "Listen, I want to tell you something. I was a Fascist right up to the end. I didn't want to see *Everybody Go Home!*, it was my daughter who made me go and see it; but I must admit that this film deeply disturbed me." Need I say more?

Manichean films, with the good guys and the bad guys, are made to get applause from those who are already convinced, and the 'boos' from those who aren't. I believe that a work of art always disturbs because it bothers the conscience, and you don't disturb with ideas but with the stimuli of the spectator's active participation in the action of a film. I don't believe in denouncing. If I make a film that denounces evil, the film will serve absolutely no purpose. However, if I bring the spectator to a certain emotional attitude and state of disturbance that make him receptive to new and different ideas, this is the little grain of sand that will be a step forward. These grains of sand are very tiny, though the sum of many little stimuli leads to results.

The Discovery of Responsibility

– *In* Everybody Go Home! *the change that comes over the leading character played by Alberto Sordi is characteristic of many of the heroes in your films. And then, another main feature of your cinema is how detailed the supporting characters are always depicted as, for example, the father in* Everybody Go Home!

– The father (Eduardo De Filippo) is similar to what his son (Alberto Sordi) was like at the beginning of the film. The son has gone on a long trip whereas the father never did and that's what makes the difference. In Eduardo's comedy, *Napoli milionaria*, which I consider a masterpiece, there's a scene I find heart-rending and extremely beautiful. This is when Eduardo, the hero, returns to Naples after having been a prisoner in Germany. The city is plunged in the black market, money, illegal dealings with the Americans. His circle of family and friends, all involved in the black market, have him sit down, give him something to eat; he wants to tell them everything he has seen, the concentration camps... But the others tell him, "Oh, forget all of that, it's the past, don't bother us, be quiet..." But he wants to tell them that he has seen mountains of corpses. "Forget all of that, eat!" I find this scene a good example on a smaller scale of what to me represents the tragedy

of all humanity, that is, its incapacity to acquire knowledge simply because it refuses to. In the same way, the father in *Everybody Go Home!* stays closed up in his shell, he doesn't grow, whereas his son experiences new feelings and perceptions that transform him. The father doesn't change, and this causes a rupture between the two characters.

– *In a way, the encounter between father and son is the son's confrontation with his own self, with the person he was before his trip.*

– The son can no longer accept the stupidity of his father's attitude, he realizes that this behavior is a dead-end. In a way, his father, shut up in his own world, helps him react: he jumps from the window and escapes.

– *The film's underlying theme is the discovery of responsibility.*

– Exactly, discovery of the responsibility of the individual. In fact, during all of the first part of the film, Sordi keeps saying, "Where are the orders?" Who's going to give me orders?" The film is divided into three parts that represent a succession of three themes: the search for orders; there aren't any orders so I'll go home. The long trip homeward when I decide to not be tempted into adventures that could jeopardize my responsibility. Death of a friend; I'm surprised to be affected, I start to think.

– *Under these circumstances, we can very well understand what Sordi does when, at the end of the film, he takes up a machine gun and goes to participate in the insurrection of Naples.*

– It's important that this happens at the end of the film when the public, after having followed Sordi's adventures, has gone deep into the soul of the character and eventually ends up seeing that he is right and agreeing with him. Moreover, it should be added, my intentions were somewhat betrayed when the film came out. This also happened with *Bread, Love and Dreams*.

The marshall arrives in a village that has problems that are new to him, problems of poverty, underdevelopment. It's not by chance that we learn in the film that he comes from a rich region, Romagna, where there aren't these kinds of difficulties. De Sica is determined not to let himself be dragged into the village's problems; he is solely interested in his own concerns, eating, making love... Indeed, he concentrates all his lecherous desires on "la bersagliera" [a female bersagliere, a light infantry-man, *Trans*]. When he goes to the young woman's [Gina Lollobrigida] house – more than anything else, he is thinking of seducing her in prison – to feed her donkey, he is confronted with poverty for the first time and realizes that he's nothing but a coward, a petty criminal, and performs the first act of generosity in his entire life: he leaves 10,000 lire under a statue of Saint Anthony. Then, unexpectedly, this act turns into a miracle. He feels overwhelmed by a miracle that he absolutely did not want to create; he only wanted, for the first time in his life, to perform an act of humanity.

Nevertheless, from that moment on, a change has come over him, he gives up the "bersagliera" [see trans. note above] – he even tries to help her marry the young man she's in love with. So, the changes are always small. It's little things that change the world, not great ambitions that, in the end, never materialize. De Sica has changed a little. Confronted with the people's innocence he was forced, despite himself, to become conscious of certain problems that at first he wanted to ignore at all costs. This seems to me to be the film's underlying message – anyway, this is what I had in mind originally. The critics considered *Bread, Love and Dreams* to be neorealism's "burial" since it didn't throw social principles in the spectators' faces.

A look at childhood traumatized by the death of a mother (Anthony Quayle, Stefano Colagrande, Simone Giannozzi). *Incompreso* by Luigi Comencini.

A classic of Italian comedy with its awkward *carabinieri* (Memmo Carotenuto and Roberto Risso) and ravishing "bersagliera", Gina Lollobrigida. Luigi Comencini's *Pane e, amore e fantasia/Bread, Love and Dreams.*

Also, another important thing: when *Bread, Love and Dreams* was released in Italy, I got some good reviews, and even a few really excellent ones. I remember that the film critics' union in Milan, that used to have free showings every Sunday morning of films of interest to workers and students, presented my film at the Corso. So this union, made up of people who really supported neorealism, didn't consider the film to be neorealism's burial. After the tremendous success of *Bread, Love and Dreams*, and after the imitations made of it, this opinion changed completely: I was called the gravedigger of neorealism. Apart from the fact that I don't consider myself powerful enough to have been able to bury neorealism, I think that neorealism came to an end for other baser, more commercial reasons.

In my opinion, the death of neorealism was caused by the fact that Italian neorealist films were never very successful. Neorealism was successful abroad, and this foreign success made it possible for us to also make a certain type of cinema. When these films were no longer popular abroad, the vein dried up and we went looking for easy success on the domestic market: we made films with middle-class heroes, comedies. And I mean all the directors, myself included. In doing so, we betrayed our original aspiration which was to talk about the poor. Over these past years, even the most politically committed films have always ignored the tragic situation of the unfortunate. When I filmed my documentary on children *(I bambini e noi)*, this experience was fundamental, above all because I re-established contact with the proletariat and sub-proletariat again, by tearing down the walls of film-makers' salons and intellectuals' cafés. I spoke about problems that neorealism had completely abandoned. Neorealism didn't die because I made *Bread, Love and Dreams* – it died because at one point its foreign success ran out, success that was the oxygen which kept it alive.

In Italy, neorealism had always had a hard time being accepted: confronted with difficult films, the public had always preferred easy, escapist movies...

Fables

– *Many of your films deal with contemporary problems in the form of a fable, for example,* The Scientific Cardplayer.

– *The Scientific Cardplayer* was a perfect fable. I consider my films to be fables, popular fables. The fable is a popular way of storytelling. *Delitto d'amore* is also a fable: I'm not interested in the technical reasons for the young girl's death. Anyway, everyone knows that deaths sometimes occur in factories: just as there are witches in fables. Here, the witch is the factory. Today, the moral fable is the most popular way of communicating with the public.

– *What did you find particularly interesting in* The Scientific Cardplayer?

– There were two things that particularly interested me: the tempting belief in a possible stroke of good luck – something that exists in all frustrated Italian social classes; and the perceptiveness of the little girl who knew that in that game no one comes out a winner. The only real path to truth is through the little girl, so I focused a great deal on this child and I think you see this. She is the one who realizes that her parents are on the road to their own ruin. She is the one who passes judgement on Sordi; it isn't Sordi in command. In the superb scene where Sordi pretends to be ill in order to justify the fact that his wife has gone to play cards with her suitor, the little girl sees through it all. Moreover, this idea that children understand more things than adults realize, is already a theme in *Proibito rubare:* the children know that the priest *needs* to believe in goodness, in man's charity, and so they do everything not to let him down. And then we find the same theme again at the end of *La finestra sul Luna Park:* the little boy fully realizes the game his father is playing in order to regain his affection. The child doesn't really believe his father is afraid of getting on the merry-go-round; though at one point he pretends to believe him, thinking: "Just the fact that you're going through all this trouble to get me to like you is so moving that I'll give you my friendship." In fact, my female characters and my child characters resemble each other. People who possess an unconscious truth, the truth of nature, understand their close ones emotionally, that is, they understand them not through reason, but through sensitivity.

– *In your films, very special relationships are often created between characters who are extremely different from each other.*

The cruel portrait of a decadent city as depicted through a Casanova discovering his power of seduction (Elisabetta Fanti, Leonard Whiting). Luigi Comencini's *Infanzia, vocazione e prime esperienze di Giacomo Casanova veneziano.*

– This is the most exciting thing: that emotional relationships go beyond ideas and reasoning... The most extraordinary thing in life is love, the deep understanding that is born between two people who, theoretically, should have absolutely nothing to say to each other. This, for example, is what characterizes *Delitto d'amore:* in theory, Nullo and Carmela have nothing in common; if it had been a computer defining the features of the ideal woman for Nullo and the ideal man for Carmela, its results would have been quite different. However, the miracle of life is the fact that there are sensations, an unconscious understanding of another person, something that this person will never be able to explain himself. The two people feel attracted to each other by a sensitivity in the second degree, an unconscious sensitivity that runs very deep.

– *We see this kind of feeling again in* Bebo's Girl.

– I'm always fascinated by this theme: how love – this is rather rhetorical – can overcome all differences. It's something irrational that comes from hidden perceptions bordering on the unconscious: an individual feels attracted to another person in a violent, forceful, overpowering way and he can't explain why. Mara is a totally apolitical young girl; and yet she senses that Bebo needs help, without actually knowing how she can help him. Nevertheless, Mara knows that by giving him her affection, she is helping him. Basically, man's tragedy is solitude and the answer to solitude is friendship or love. It is precisely this incommunicability, that Antonioni so often spoke of, that is destroyed by that mysterious something we call friendship or love – better still, it's called love.

– *As for friendship, we find this kind of relationship between Nino Manfredi and Mario Adorf in* Jail Break.

– Yes, that's true. At the end of the film, Manfredi nevertheless betrays Adorf, though reluctantly and with great pain, because he is forced to. The relationship between Geppetto and Pinocchio can be analyzed in the same perspective. Pinocchio does everything he can to upset Geppetto, and the latter is overcome with despair. Nevertheless, not only does Geppetto love Pinocchio, but Pinocchio, deep down inside, loves his father, too, and is sorry that he makes his father so unhappy. Pinocchio can't help himself, since just the fact that he's a child drives him to rebel against his parents.

– *Children always have to challenge their parents.*

– I think this is how it should be. The important thing in life is that each person plays his role. The role of parents is to try to be loved by their children. Children love and reject their parents: it's an obvious tragedy. Such a difficult, complex relationship makes many people believe that the family is a thing of the past. But the family possesses this conflict in a natural way, the family is the seat of conflict but this conflict is vital, not fatal. Vital conflicts are those which possess that mysterious spark called love which serves as a bedrock for confrontations; fatal conflicts are those where love doesn't exist. The search for a father figure isn't the search for authority, but for a model of behaviour. And thus, I really defend the premise that paternity, the contrary of maternity – and even for maternity though I don't really know to what point – is something acquired, not something determined by blood. I could very well be a father to my son's friend, whereas my own son could very well not recognize me as his father since I have never created the kind of relationship that comes not only out of living together, but also from a human relationship built up day after day.

Delitto d'amore *(1973)*

– *You referred to* Delitto d'amore *as a fable.*

– Yes, because it wasn't a realistic film. If I had wanted to do a documentary or make a realistic film about factory deaths caused by poisoning, the topic would have had to have been more specific. Fables, as a way of alluding to specific problems, are just as effective though they treat these problems, as I do, by way of a seemingly romantic story that ends with a moral.

The film has been criticized for its lack of realism: why doesn't anyone realize that there's such a harmful atmosphere in the factory? Why don't the workers band together? Why didn't they go on strike

On the set of *Cuore,* Luigi Comencini discusses with the venerable master of Neapolitan theater, here in the role of a retired schoolmaster, Eduardo De Filippo.

before the catastrophe? I was also asked to specifically name the lethal poison. And, since people have often reproached me about how easily the young woman seems to die, I might add that it's not the way she dies that matters, but rather the fact that she does die. I gathered several press clippings on the problem of the noxiousness in factories and just recently in *Corriere della Sera* there was a particularly shocking article: "The cancer factory continues to reap victims. With the three deaths in recent months, the number of workers who have died at the factory in Chieri near Turin has now reached forty victims, with eighty people reporting lesions. The illness results in cancer of the bladder. One hundred employees still work in the varnish and paint plants. The owners have been accused of unintentional manslaughter with aggravating circumstances."

So, deaths in these factories are not only the result of the poisonous air that causes diseases, but also of products that are sometimes violently toxic. There is a very widespread phenomenon being reported in the press: people are dying in factories. My film is a fable since when we reach a certain point, the young girl dies. The girl's death perhaps has a more romantic side, too, since, in my opinion, she also dies from her incapacity to adapt – like an animal from Africa when put in a European zoo dies, though we can't really say why. The film is not only about the harmfulness of the air breathed in factories, it also deals with the theme of cruelty towards the poor. This cruelty exists at different levels, including cultural uprooting, which makes displaced persons of these people. Their displacement creates neuroses and keeps them from reacting, from resisting. Thus at times people aren't killed by something from outside, but let themselves die: this is, in a way, what happens to the young girl, since she never struggles violently, but lets herself die almost as if she had wanted to.

– *In the clash between Nullo and Carmela, we see that the South's culture is never represented negatively.*

– I've never wanted to contrast a backward South with a more modern, more advanced North. In my opinion, culture is culture: there is no backward culture and advanced culture. African culture of the black races before the arrival of the whites was an extremely respectable culture, not backward, but different. The true culture of the South, not the one distorted by the colonization of the North, by industrialization, is a rich culture. Moreover, it has produced artists, poets, musicians, singers... Southern tradition is very important. Northern workers' modernism, in itself very respectable, resulted more out of political progress than cultural progress. Popular roots have been lost and every-

After having often focused on children, Comencini takes a look at the solitude of the aged (Michel Serrault and Virna Lisi). Luigi Comencini's *Buon natale, Buon anno/Merry Christmas, Happy New Year.*

thing has been levelled off into a kind of consumer mentality, which has also taken over the working class. In Petri's film, *The Working Class Goes to Heaven,* this is expressed very clearly by the beautiful scene in which Volonté, left alone in his apartment after his wife has left him, makes an inventory of all the useless objects in the house.

– Do you see a solution to the problems of domestic emigration?

– But what solution is there at the moment in Italy? Everything has been destroyed. Today there is not one solution to any of Italy's problems. We have reached such a disastrous point that any hope of improvement is purely theoretical.

– There is a profound feeling of despair in the film. Even Nullo's act, when he goes to murder his boss in the factory, is an act of despair.

– It's almost a symbolic act. His feeling still finds its resolution within the bounds of a one-to-one relationship. The problem was created above all – this is a very complex issue – by Italy's industrialization,

that transformed it from an agricultural into an industrial country, and which was carried out in a savagely capitalistic way that very quickly depleted the resources of an inexpensive labor force. Entrepreneurs showed an ingenious cleverness in setting about producing all kinds of useless things for which there naturally would not have been an unlimited market indefinitely, and this ran the gamut from cars to electrical appliances. In addition, bringing southern labor to the North was a catastrophe. Turin, for instance, was a peaceful city with barely one million inhabitants: now the city is worse than Chicago. Why? Because factories ideally should have been set up where the labor force was, instead of having people from the South go to the North to work in new plants. This discussion can go pretty far. In my television documentary series, *I bambini e noi,* one of the programs was devoted to problems of domestic emigration and emigration abroad, to the problems of families split up because the father worked in the North or in Germany.

– Nullo is a member of the Communist Party. One of the scenes in the film takes place in the Antonio

Gramsci communist branch. What was the role of the Italian Communist Party in the social context described in the film?

– I'm not a communist, and so I don't really know from the inside what the Communist Party's detailed policy is regarding these problems. The party neglected the southern issue; it realized this later and now is trying to correct this negligence. Since it was easier to organize the northern workers, who were true proletarians, the sub-proletariat of the South was left to fend for itself. This was one of the Communist Party's mistakes: it left the South in the hands of reactionaries, and thus we are now faced with a fascist South. In the North – I shot *Delitto d'amore* in Cinisello Balsamo, a small town near Milan with a Communist municipal council and a very nice mayor (who even helped me with some shots) – the problem was that the C.P. was powerful in the big companies, in the unions. In small companies, it's difficult to get people together: the workers are elusive, they're more vulnerable to blackmail from their bosses. Southerners, in fact, live with the constant threat of being laid off. Political action is made very difficult because of the mixture of northern and southern workers that exists, that is, between proletarians and the new workers who have come from the sub-proletariat; the latter are full of contradictions just like the young girl in the film. They are extremely attached to their traditions and have a suspicious attitude.

– Through the character of the factory doctor you were able to allude to management paternalism.

– This character was created while the script was being written. The factory in the film is a combination of different factories: no factory manager would ever have accepted to have his plant appear officially as a place where people had died. The particulars such as the doctor's office, the changing rooms and toilets, where that strange love scene takes place, are all from a different factory than the one where the machines are. This was a dye factory – a factory where the noxiousness in the air was very strong – that seemed very modern, efficient, very well designed, even in terms of its medical facilities.

There's an anecdote I'd like to tell you. For the factory scene, we needed little masks that the female workers, at one point, were supposed to wear: when Nullo sees these masks he realizes that there is a danger of poisoning and he suddenly understands why Carmela isn't feeling well. Nullo goes to the doctor with this mask, reproaching him and crying, "Murderer!" The masks we were using for the film weren't special in any way: we had bought them in a store in Rome and they were normally meant for auto workers who painted cars. In the factory where we shot the scene of the workers wearing these masks, there was a woman doctor in charge of the medical department. After having watched us shoot the scene she asked me,"Where did you buy those masks?" "In a store in Rome where they sell rubber articles." I thought she was asking me this in order to comment on an incorrect technical detail or to tell me that the masks were useless. Instead, on the contary, she then asked me to give her the masks: "I'd like to see if these masks might be useful to the factory workers who are subject to high intoxication," she explained. This was an astonishing thing to hear in a factory that seemed so modern, efficient and yet...

– The scene about the contaminated river poses the problem of pollution.

– This problem is very serious. In this environment people breathe a physical as well as moral poison. When I saw the contaminated river, it was the Ambro near Milan, it came as a real surprise to me. I knew that rivers in Lombardy had become polluted cesspools, but had never imagined that things had deteriorated to such a point. I remembered the streams where I used to go swimming as a child. All of Lombardy was a very rich agricultural region since it was thoroughly irrigated by a perfect system of canals, a system created by Leonardo da Vinci. Today, these wonderful facilities are unusable since the water is polluted: farmers can't water their crops with that water anymore.

– How was the film received in Italy?

– In Italy the film was utterly torn apart. I still wonder today how there could have been such a combination of circumstances that resulted in the failure of the film. This film filled me with bitterness. They released it at the wrong time; I had wanted it to be released in October. Instead, they made me edit the film in a hurry and then released it in April. That was too late in Italy for a sensitive, delicate film, which at the same time was serious, committed. On April 20 only a popular film could be released, one that would have a chance of continuing a first run all the way through September. In that case, it could have continued being shown all the next year. When a film only has a first run from April 20 to May 10, the film is finished. After that, *Delitto d'amore* was never shown again, not even one day in Rome. What was worse, the film received bad reviews from the left-wing journalists – something that really surprised me. Here, again, we were up against an old issue: if films weren't intellectual, they weren't left-wing. Simple stories weren't any good because they were popular and, therefore, too easy. For all of these reasons the film was taken out of distribution..

– *Even from a political point of view I think that choosing popular cinema as a means of dealing with serious problems is a good approach.*

– I think so too. But no, it's not right... So, for a film like *Delitto d'amore,* the situation was very difficult. A film must be a huge success in order to survive. In this respect the critics are somewhat responsible. Critics always look down on popular films, comic films.

(SECOND INTERVIEW)

Traffic Jam *(1979)*

– *You had been thinking about this film for a long time, hadn't you?*

– Ever since 1972, I had this rather confused idea about making a film that takes place entirely in a traffic jam; I thought this traffic jam would perfectly symbolize the situation in which we find ourselves today. The screenplay had been ready for two years. I based the shooting, however, on a screenplay that I rewrote twice before starting the filming. The first producer who got the screenplay couldn't make the film for lack of financing in Italy. The film was passed on to another producer who in turn passed it on to a third. The deal was finally put together thanks to a co-production with France, Spain, Germany and Italy.

– *In writing the story for* Traffic Jam *did you use things which you had read before?*

– No, the story was completely new. The closest you can come to it is, if you remember, there was a traffic jam at the beginning of *8 1/2*. In *Nashville,* too, there was a traffic jam, but Altman's film hadn't come out yet when I wrote the story for *Traffic Jam.* Also the stories, themes, and characters underwent a lot of change from the original story to the completed film. The only thing that remained throughout and right up to the end, was that I wanted to make a film that started out in a realistic way – basically like the way Italian comedies do – and then that gradually slipped into the fantastic – and also the dramatic and frightening.

– *In its symbolic dimension, it seems to me that we can draw certain analogies between* Traffic Jam *and* The Scientific Cardplayer.

– *The Scientific Cardplayer* is a modern fable, a special fable: a little girl poisons a witch. Fables always have an ending. However, what characterizes *Traffic Jam*, is that it doesn't have an ending. Here, there is no solution; the film ends with a question mark. *Quatre de l'infanterie* ends with 'The End' followed by a question mark. In *Traffic Jam,* you need a question mark without 'The End.'

– *Wasn't this desperate ending partially responsible for the Italian public's lukewarm response?*

– The film's relative failure in Italy should be seen from different angles. There was the problem of the film's presentation to the public; this encounter got off on the wrong foot because of the advertising, and also because the critics didn't exercise the little influence they could have had upon the public. In order to get the financing, I had to use too many famous actors. In the beginning, I didn't want even one star to play any of the parts. I was only thinking in terms of Mastroianni, but his appearance was justified since in fact he was playing his own self; so we needed a star. The French producer agreed to invest under the condition that we used four famous French actors or actresses – in the end these turned out to be Annie Girardot, Miou Miou, Gérard Depardieu,

Comencini prepares a film shot while the actors look on.

Patrick Dewaere – after which, to balance these out, the Italian producer then imposed his own Italian stars. This line-up of famous actors made the public expect a typical Italian comedy, that is, a film which can be satirical and carries some bite, but in which the underlying rapport with the spectator is still laughs, irony. The public found this to be true at the beginning of the film, then the satirical and comical tone disappeared and there was a certain disappointment when the story shifted into alarming situations, such as the scene when the young girl is raped, and finally, to the film's problematic ending. It represented a difficult kind of relationship with the public. I think that the duty of the critics – at least of a certain kind of critic – would have been to support a film that was new and different. *Traffic Jam* was a break with traditional Italian comedy where everything always ended in a big toast around the table. I'm convinced that by always rehashing the same things, Italian comedy sort of encouraged an indifference towards Italian social problems. By turning everything into a joke, in the end everything is forgiven. In my opinion, Italian comedy destroyed its function, a function that it indisputably had.

As for the critics, they were put off by all the famous actors and actresses: they saw this as an effort to score a big commercial success. Success is the thing that really puts off Italian critics the most. I remember the time when *Everybody Go Home!* didn't receive the Quality Award and one of the members on the committee declared – someone told me this later – "An award for quality shouldn't be given to a film with Alberto Sordi in it; Sordi is a popular actor." Basically, there's this dividing line: someone who uses Sordi is doing business, someone who doesn't use him is creating art. And so, all of these famous actors – popular actors, in fact – had two negative consequences: the first, to prepare the public for a type of film that they were going to see; the second, to put off the critics who, instead of defending the film, considered it an Italian comedy with pretentions and ambitions that were inappropriate to it, that even perhaps weren't considered appropriate to comedy nor to the author himself. A comedy, which had been made very professionally but that had nothing special about it such as *Il gatto,* got better reviews than *Traffic Jam. Traffic Jam* was one of the rare films, perhaps the seven or eight, that I've made with a tremendous desperate will to make them. When you think that in Italy films such as *Infanzia, vocazione e prime esperienze di Giacomo Casanova veneziano* or *Mio Dio, come sono caduta in basso!* were completely ignored by the critics... The critics more or less accepted the latter simply because of the charm of the comedy, but no one discussed whether the hypothesis of a satire on D'Annunzio's ideas should be accepted or refused: "D'Annunzio is Visconti's area, not Comencini's!"

The film was funny and that was enough for the critics, but what I really wanted to express wasn't important in the least. Nor did anyone bring up what I was trying to do in *Infanzia, vocazione e prime esperienze di Giacomo Casanova veneziano.*

– *Why is it that the characters played by Tognazzi, Miou Miou and Depardieu only make their appearance in the middle of the film?*

– It wasn't like that in the screenplay. Having such great actors – nevertheless paid at reasonable fees – meant that I only had them for very short periods. I therefore had to study the times the characters were together and shoot with only some of them some of the time, and others at other times. For example, the group Miou Miou, Depardieu, Tognazzi was hired for five days and we had very bad weather for all of that time. So, I had to have them appear in the evening instead, though in the screenplay they were supposed to arrive before, with their story having other implications. Anyway, I'm only telling you this to give you an idea, it's not at all a justification.

I had to really fight with the producer so that he wouldn't impose even more stars. For example, for the final monologue of the woman whose child has been asleep for six years, he kept saying, "I'll get you Sophia Loren, Claudia Cardinale..." I told him, "Don't come and bother me anymore about this, I want an unknown." And, in fact, the actress who plays the role was a woman who just happened to be there at the time and who had never acted before. I asked her to play the part. *Traffic Jam* should have been entirely done like that, with genuine, right faces.

– *Given all the characters and situations, how did you manage to work it all out in the end?*

– The screenplay called for a final catastrophe: a toxic cloud was supposed to appear and all the drivers die. On paper this sequence seemed alright, but as always – and this is something I continually see – there is no connection between the written word and the image – they are two completely different languages. So, anyway, I started shooting this general asphyxiation – and very soon realized that the whole thing was completely ridiculous. You can write that John Doe dies locked in his car, but seeing the face of a dead Tognazzi, are two different things. And, moreover, this ending was too simplistic as a catastrophe. I just didn't like the idea. So, I started wondering how the film should really end. I recalled the story of a woman whose child had been asleep for six years. This was a story I had in my papers – I had mountains of things written about the traffic jam idea that were never used – and this woman seemed both symbolic and realistic at the same time. In using this woman's monologue for the end of the film, I felt I was bringing together two things: on the one hand, a type of allegory, an image of trust, of irrational confidence – this woman wanted only one thing, and that was to hear her child's voice again, she was oblivious to anything else happening in the world, and she kept believing in life – and on the other hand, by a return to reality with the impossibility of dispelling the traffic jam despite the good news broadcast on the radio. So I used this scene for the ending and it seems right, it works. After that, a helicopter arrives announcing that the traffic jam is clearing and asks the drivers to get back into their cars. In fact, it's a false alarm. The engines start up, then are turned off, no one leaves, silence falls over the scene. No one speaks, you hear a few weak honkings but even these are finally hushed.

– *Beyond the comic elements,* Traffic Jam *is a frightening, desperate film. In this regard, it expresses a theme that appears constantly throughout your work.*

– It's really not necessary to have a lot of imagination to be frightened, all you have to do is read the newspapers – all over the world. I really don't know what we can still hope for. What hope do we have? Nothing but this mother who wants to hear her child's voice in order to keep hoping. I have never made any optimistic films; I made light comedies that were falsely optimistic such as *Bread, Love and...* I made ironic movies that might have thrown a little wink. Even my first film, *Proibito rubare,* wasn't optimistic, it was even the complete opposite of what optimism might have inspired. *Traffic Jam* wasn't made lightheartedly, it was a film that meant a great deal to me.

Mario Monicelli

– In your career as filmmaker you got your start directing movies starring Totò, films you made in association with Steno. Among these works, I find Totò cerca casa *particularly successful; I think it's a very good film.*

– Let's not exaggerate, more than being a very good film, it was a farce. Farces are always wonderful because they're very hard to make; they're a season of life that can never be repeated. The farce is an extraordinary genre, it represents something that is lost and is difficult to ever recover again; American farces of the silent era have a charm and beauty that it's impossible to reproduce. Nevertheless, when shooting this type of film, they're made spontaneously, with great passion, simplicity, innocence, on everyone's part: the producer, screenwriter, director, actors. Thirty years later, when we see these films again, they've become good films but, in fact, let's be truthful, they aren't really always. They have the beauty of fresh newness, of off-handedness, which if you like, might even be considered a style. Concerning *Totò cerca casa,* you could say that for the first time here was a farce whose theme dealt with a burning social issue, the theme of the housing shortage in Italy, a very serious problem at the time. Instead of making dramas on the subject like everyone else, we made the film in a naturally burlesque style. In a way, this is what gave birth to comic films or farces related to reality, daily existence. In a certain sense, with *Totò cerca casa,* we see the buddings of the "Italian" comedy: the linking of the comic, the amusing, the satirical to a criticism of manners, to social reality, these had their origins a little in that film.

In fact, the film that was really based upon a serious theme was *Cops and Robbers.* It was here that a particular type of Italian comic film emerged and not only just a well-constructed farce. *Cops and Robbers* had a solid structure, the story was by Tellini and the screenplay was written by Flaiano, Brancati, Steno and myself. The idea was good and, with Totò and Aldo Fabrizi, it had a certain structure already, it was already a genuine Italian comedy, a comedy of manners. Totò was directed in a different way, not only along the lines of the farce, but with a human side. In the story of this thief and policeman, there

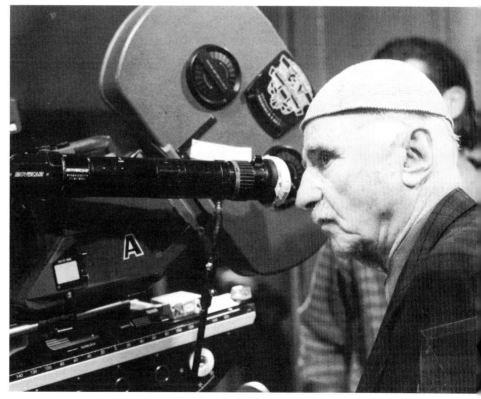

A specialist in Italian comedy, a great filmmaker with a career of exceptional longevity, Mario Monicelli.

Mel Ferrer (with Marco Guglielmi, left) in one of his rare films made in Italy, based on a Sardinian drama by Grazia Deledda and brought to the screen in 1954 by Mario Monicelli, *Proibito*.

was already some bitterness, it was no longer simply a farce – to which, I repeat, I am very attached and which I respect very much – it was another genre, it was a comedy. The film was a big success, but at the time it caused a real scandal. I was summoned by the Director General of the Department of Entertainment since it was considered revolutionary to show that it was possible for a policeman and a thief to become friends, that they could share common problems. They helped each other out and, in the end, when the thief was taken to prison, he reminded the policeman to take care of his family for him. Putting these two people on the same level seemed revolutionary, as if the foundations of Italian society had been shaken. We have to remember that five years earlier, Italy was still under Fascism.

– *I think that* Totò e Carolina *had even greater problems with the censors.*

– They really massacred Totò e Carolina. The sto-

ry of this young girl who wanted to commit suicide and who in fact only found help, comfort and comprehension from the Communists, could only displease the censors. The Church, the police, the family, all of these Catholics were indifferent; however some Communists on their way to a demonstration with their red flags come to her rescue. The Minister of Interior seemed like he had gone completely crazy; here again it also seemed I had placed a bomb under Italy – to depict Communists as human and comprehensive, to show the red flag... The film was blocked for a year and a half and then, when it was released, it had undergone thirty-four cuts! At that time, we weren't free to speak about anything really, but the government, the *carabinieri*, the police force, were absolutely off limits. If we made a film about a rather crooked lawyer, the association of lawyers would lodge a complaint against us and it would be heard. The Ministry summoned us. It was a continuous battle. Fortunately, we pushed – I don't mean just Steno and myself, but all of the Italian film world – we pushed so that things would become more transparent. Little by little, we managed to achieve our present position.

– The period you're talking about was the one that witnessed the death of neorealism. It was the terrible early fifties.

– This was when there was a real climate of Catholic conformity, a frustrating climate of insinuations, of things concealed by the Christian Democrats. Cinema, which was mass entertainment – in Italy, in those days, audiences were at an all-time high – was monitored particularly closely; the authorities kept after it relentlessly. Nevertheless, I must admit that these were also very stimulating years because we were struggling a lot and there were really some courageous producers: they made it possible for us to make them, these films that ran into problems with the censors; they didn't hesitate to invest their money. Ponti, de Laurentiis, Cristaldi

were also young; they, too, wanted to confront certain problems. Now we've all become conformists, especially the producers who are loaded and no longer want to take any risks. Before, they didn't have a penny and they produced films that would maybe never have been made. Today they have millions and they only want to produce sure bets. That's the way it is, unfortunately.

– It seems then that there was a time when Italian cinema also owed its strength to producers.

– Indeed the support producers gave to film directors should be recognized. The producer was an ally, he was committed to the film that was being made, he defended the director against the distributor and the cinema owner. Today there's a dictatorship of the distributor; he always demands the same product, a product that he wants to correspond to what cinema owners want. In my opinion, one of the disturbing aspects of the present crisis of Italian cine-

On the set of the Italian comedy classic, *I soliti ignoti/Big Deal on Madonna Street,* **Mario Monicelli (woolen bonnet) prepares a scene with his actors, Vittorio Gassman, Totò, Renato Salvatori and, partly hidden, Marcello Mastroianni.**

A painful evoking of World War I in the guise of a comedy, Alberto Sordi and Vittorio Gassman in Mario Monicelli's *La grande guerra/The Great War.*

ma is the fact that there aren't any young producers. It's not enough to have young film directors – I'm talking about directors in the their twenties – there's a lack of producers who are prepared to listen to them. There are young people with ideas, who have things to say, current things, things that concern their generation, their problems. There are also screenwriters, actors... and they are all obliged to turn to producers who are old. I find this very serious: if no new producers appear this can really be an obstacle to a new kind of Italian cinema being born. We've been making movies for thirty years now and we've become old. We're all in our sixties, and there has been a generation in between, people in their forties, that have gone completely bankrupt. This was perhaps a little our fault, but I think it was also a lot theirs, too: they had nothing to say except what we were already saying ourselves and we knew how to

say it better than anyone else. And so here came a whole lot of Antonionis, Fellinis, Viscontis and even Monicellis: they wanted to say things the way we did and so were crushed. However, the generation of those in their twenties is essential: they want to say things that are completely different, in a way we know nothing about. Relationships are different, their writing is different: today, in my opinion, this is the only way to win back the public, a public that we held for thirty years by modifying our ways of doing things, by very cleverly following all the changes in cinema. Perhaps even now, with our skillfulness, we are still capable of adapting; however, this comes spontaneously to these young people and this is something we don't know how to do. Nevertheless, they need to be given the chance to express themselves and this is something they don't have, since producers don't have confidence in them.

We are witnessing a new rise of American cinema, and there are two reasons for this: first of all, because there's this slacking off of Italian cinema. Up to a few years ago, Italian cinema was very strong and had successfully ousted American films from the Italian market. Afterwards, the Americans learned to make movies modeled after European cinema. They had remained closed up in the studios while we had gone out into the streets to film the man on the street. Today, they have a generation of filmmakers who have learned to work in this way. If the Americans have learned, with the possibilities that they have, with their force and power, with their knowledge of problems that are of such prime importance compared with our own, it is obvious that we will be crushed. If they make a satirical film about the President, it's the President of the United States, certainly it's not the President of Italy or even the President of France – with all respect due to France. The important thing is that they've come out of the studios, and that they've begun making films like the ones we've been making for years in Italy, in France and even in England, and thus successfully "beat us at our own game." It's not the "disaster" films that we should be afraid of, since these have always existed. The same goes for the James Bond series; these films were tremendously successful, but American cinema was inexistent apart from them: Italian cinema had completely swept it away. The various Altmans or Scorseses are today the ones who are really a threat since they make European-style films, Italian style...

– *Even in your earliest films your taste for choosing inexperienced actors is evident, new faces, or using famous players in roles that are unusual for them.*

– I've always had a lot of fun using new actors, sometimes even actors off the street – but this wasn't only me, it was part of neorealism. I also had fun taking actors and using them in a completely different way than what was habitual for them: I did this again recently with Alberto Sordi in *A Very Little Man.* Sordi is a comic actor and I had him play a very tragic role, very rough even. I did the same thing, inversely, with Vittorio Gassman and

Monica Vitti. I like doing this, it's a way of expression that helps me; I use it in order to say many things. Moreover, the film director's job – no one really knows very well what it is, least of all the journalists who ask the same questions about content, as if that were the only thing that existed. But a film director's job is also choosing locations; this is a very important part of directing, just as casting is essential, and the desire to use them in a different way, to take them out of their normal mode. Directing doesn't only consist of moving the camera around. The camera's movements are the least important; in fact, the very great film directors never move the camera. Just to give you another example, in *Caro Michele,* I had Lou Castel, who had always played violent characters, also in westerns, act a rather weak and quiet homosexual. In my opinion, he's this character to a T, he achieves extraordinary perfection. I was able to grasp another side of his personality, something that was the opposite of anything he had ever been asked to do. Again, this is part of being a director and yet it is still ignored, something no one ever speaks about. A film director is also this, better still, he is perhaps above all this. Taking a place, a person, transforming them, seeing them in a new way, this is the job of a director, this is the joy he should have in making a movie. His work is not only in terms of the movie's content, which critics hammer away at relentlessly. The materials that the director uses also give birth to content. Directing consists above all in getting various components to work, putting elements together such as actors, objects, places, a certain kind of photography. This is what is really important in directing, and no one ever mentions it; it's as if it didn't exist. People talk about the meaning of each scene, the characters' psychology, to show how such-and-such a situation could never have happened. This is useless since anything can be done, everything is possible, all psychologies are acceptable. Critics all take themselves to be great masters, all of them want to explain how the film director should do things, how the feelings between the characters should develop. This is all rubbish: all psychologies are valid as long as they're expressed in the right way. Critics should see films analyzing the details of the image, the details of the different components of the image; instead, they see these only in terms of the details of the screenplay.

– You are rather bitter when it comes to critics.

– Yes, because critics are always and only concerned about the screenplay. A critic is always and only a writer who is only interested in other writers and in deciding how well or not they have written the screenplay. However, a film is something else. Critics are only concerned with the potential novel alongside the film, never with the image of the novel. It is the succession of images that gives its substance to a filmic tale; it's nothing else, this is the nature of a story, a film is told in images.

– Before shooting a film, you devote a lot of time to choosing the actors and searching for locations.

– For me the most exhausting part of a film is the preparation, that is, the choice of places and faces, since this is when everything that has been thought and written takes shape. There's nothing more exhausting or depressing. When you've made the right choices, the shooting always goes well. When you're in the right place with the right actors, shooting poses no problem.

– For example, I believe in A Very Little Man *you took great pains in choosing the neighborhood where Alberto Sordi's apartment was located. This shot alone already gives meaning to the film.*

– With the film's set designer, Lorenzo Baraldi, the two of us took two and a half months to find this apartment, we took photos, we saw a thousand things. I was aware that this shot would be the one to give a certain tone to the film. Everything else was also chosen with great care. So, I devote an enormous amount of time to finding locations. If I didn't, the shooting wouldn't be very good. If I find myself in a place that isn't right – that happens sometimes – I realize it later when I find it hard to shoot, I don't feel at ease, I'm not happy, I start getting nervous, start getting angry quickly. People wonder why, and me too, I ask myself, and then realize that I can't find the right way to shoot a scene, that the place isn't right, that I've made a mistake. Let's not even go into when it's a mistake in the

choice of an actor; the shooting then becomes a real nightmare. Sometimes the problem can come from a mistake in the way the screenplay is written. For example – just to cite a famous movie, one where it's easy to confirm what I'm going to say – the end of *Big Deal on Madonna Street* was very different than what was finally shot. The first ending didn't work; I couldn't find the location to shoot it. We started the filming and I didn't know what to do. Finally, I advised the producer Franco Cristaldi, I stopped the shooting for two days and, with Age and Scarpelli we rewrote the final sequence. Not being able to find the right location for the last sequence meant that something wasn't working in the screenplay and vice versa: things all rely upon each other a lot. With the new ending – we came up with the idea that after knocking through the wall, not only do they find themselves in the kitchen, which was already in the screenplay, but also instead of opening the safe, they open the refrigerator and end up talking about spaghetti and beans. It was lacking something, we needed a grand finale for this comedy which was also full of bitterness. Once this sequence was written, with the heroes eating and talking a little about their lives, I had no problem whatsoever ending the film nor finding the place where they go their own ways.

Before starting to shoot I also choose the supporting actors very carefully. In a movie, when the casting is right for second-level and even third-level actors, the film has a different tone, it corresponds exactly to what you've wanted to do. Even for a barman who serves coffee, I never take the first person who comes by; though I don't spend months on it, I do try out several people before deciding. For certain roles I also like to use non-professional actors. I do this often, for example in *Caro Michele,* there's poet Alfonso Gatto and film director Fabio Carpi. It's not only me who does this; it's something quite customary in Italian cinema; that started with Rossellini, Pasolini.

– During the fifties you shot almost all comedies with one exception: Proibito.

– I never wanted to make a dramatic film, really dramatic, the only one was *Proibito*. First of all, it doesn't come naturally to me, I don't want to say things in a dramatic way, I don't like to, it seems dated, old-fashioned. I don't know... it doesn't seem very modern to want to always express yourself solely through drama. And then, with my disposition, I like saying things a little tongue-in-cheek, or at least with a satirical intention, with a desire to ridicule. *Proibito* was an experiment I made and which confirmed to me that it wasn't in my nature to express things only in a dramatic way. My films, in fact, have always alternated comic moments with dramatic moments, even very dramatic. My real inspiration is to contin-

ually put these two modes together, to even combine farce and tragedy. I have always tried to do this, sometimes it has turned out well, other times not; but there's always been this mixture, *Big Deal on Madonna Street, The Great War, The Organizer, L'armata Brancaleone, Amici miei, A Very Little Man...* Basically, theorizing a little, in life things are like that. But anyway, I don't want to make a general theory out of my way of seeing things.

– The Great War *seems to me one of the films that best reveals this type of approach. Moreover, just*

A grotesque tone to portray workers' struggles at the end of the last century, Marcello Mastroianni in Mario Monicelli's *I compagni/The Organizer.*

Comedy of manners on the wane, Monica Vitti deserts Antonioni's films with Carlo Giuffré in Mario Monicelli's *La ragazza con la pistola/Girl With a Gun*.

as importantly, the film deals with the theme of the war of 1915-1918 in a realistic way, not commemorative, and this was a first in Italian cinema.

– In Italy it was forbidden, and not only in movies, but also in the theater, in the press, to talk about the Great War other than by exalting the soldiers, the heroes who had gone to fight the Austrians to retake Trento and Trieste: "Italy is engaged in the final war of independence." When news appeared that I wanted to make a film on the Great War with Alberto Sordi and Vittorio Gassman, the newspapers – *Il Giorno, Il Corriere della Sera* – published feature articles written by important journalists saying that the film should be banned. Even before shooting had commenced there was a campaign against the film: "Sordi, Gassman, Monicelli, Age, Scarpelli will only defile the six hundred thousand who died in World War I." Once the film was released, it was total rupture. A film could finally say that these men had gone to war without knowing why; the war hadn't concerned them, Italy didn't exist, nothing existed. They

were just poor devils, badly dressed, badly fed, ignorant, illiterate, who had gone to do a job that had nothing to do with them. So this was the idea I wanted to give of the Great War. I also wanted – this is something I didn't manage to do successfully – not to have just one hero, but to have an indistinct mass from which, from time to time, a character would emerge, a character who would make us laugh, another who would make us cry, a third who would die, and so on. But then, after it was completed, it was a film with two actors. I had hoped that Sordi and Gassman would blend in more with the others. As far as the screenplay was concerned, I believed that it was feasible, but while shooting it was impossible, despite the presence of quite a lot of characters, to not focus on the heroes. It should also be said that with Sordi's and Gassman's personalities, it would have been a difficult undertaking... I had waged a long battle with the producers about how the film would end: they found it unacceptable that the film ends tragically, that it would finish in defeat. For me, however, it was essential that the two men be shot. I had already had to struggle to impose the endings of *Cops and Robbers* and that of *Big Deal on Madonna Street.* My desire to often end my films, if not in a tragic, at least in a bitter way, is really part of how I perceive things. My heroes are unfortunate men who throw themselves into undertakings that are completely over their heads: this may seem funny, but it is essentially tragic. The theme based upon a search for the impossible, which is unattainable because one lacks the necessary means, has often been treated in my films, in *Cops and Robbers, The Organizer, L'armata Brancaleone, Brancaleone alle crociate,* and even as early as *Totò cerca casa.* In short, the attempt to do something greater than oneself and in the end the failure and the frustration.

– The Great War *was very successful whereas* The Organizer, *which dealt with workers' struggles in a similar perspective, was a commercial failure. What do you attribute this to?*

– The film did very badly. It had all the ingredients to be a success, and even a great success. I'm convinced that five years later it would have been very well received. It was a film before its time, that came when people didn't feel like hearing about these problems; it seemed like a Communist propaganda movie about the working class. And yet the film had comical parts, it had been made in the usual way with that mixture of funny and tragic elements; it was therefore a particularly difficult film, it was in the same vein as *The Great War.* Perhaps the word "comrades" frightened people; those were the days of the center-left in Italy. Whatever the case may be, the public didn't go to see the film.

Second sequel to a memorable saga: following *L'armata Brancaleone, Brancaleone alle crociate* takes our hero as far as the Holy Land (Vittorio Gassman, Paolo Villaggio, Lino Toffolo, all kneeling).

Ordinary drama of a petty bourgeois who, taking justice in his hands, becomes a murderer. Alberto Sordi, Shelley Winters, Vincenzo Crociti in Mario Monicelli's *Un borghese piccolo piccolo/A Very Little Man.*

– Was it you who chose to make a film out of such a story?

– The Organizer was one of the rare films that was really my idea from the start. I remember that one evening in Paris – I don't know why we were in Paris – I was walking back to the hotel with Franco Cristaldi and I said to him, "I want to make a film on a strike that failed, on how the strike is created and why it is unsuccessful; I'd like to show the contradictions, the pathetic and ridiculous sides..." Since I had already made several films with Cristaldi – he knew me well, he knew that I knew how to make this kind of film, with lots of characters, lots of episodes – he immediately told me he liked the idea. And this was how the film came to be and how I got the chance to say a certain number of things I felt strongly about. I wanted to say that

strikes came about spontaneously, that strikes were inevitable in a given situation, that there were men capable of uniting and refusing to work in order to obtain certain concessions, to go on strike accepting the risks that this involved. I wanted to show why under certain conditions a strike cannot *not* happen; there was a search for truth and even a justification for the occupying of factories. When Mastroianni arrives on the premises, he asks the comrades to attack the factory: the outline of his harangue is taken from Mark Antony's speech in Shakespeare's *Julius Caesar.* We used its arguments: while writing the scene, I had Shakespeare's text by my side. Mastroianni at first says bravo, you're right, you're doing the right thing not to go to the factory and then, little by little, he completely reverses everything.

In this film I especially wanted to say that what's

important is to be united; if things go wrong, it's not important. The hero was going to go to prison but he had succeeded in kindling hope. Of course, it's a bit didactic. For example, the scene where the torch is passed from hand to hand is also a little didactic. I shot this knowing that there was a little social realism in it; but when things are done well, it's not a problem.

– L'armata Brancaleone *seemed meant to be mainly entertaining, but in fact it was a film that attempted to be an unconventional treatment of the Middle Ages.*

A gun in his hand (though Samuel Fuller might come to mind; this is the arm that kills Vincenzo Crocitti during a hold-up), Mario Monicelli on the set of *Un borghese piccolo piccolo/A Very Little Man.*

– I think that *L'armata Brancaleone* is the most important film that I've ever made, even more than *The Organizer.* This film was intuition. I consider it important because it was a film absolutely without precedent in film history, and not only in the history of Italian cinema. Usually there's this image of the Middle Ages, that period of the early Middle Ages shown in iconography, painting, novels, films, in school courses, as a time of knights, damsels, of Roland, a completely manneristic vision. *L'armata Brancaleone* was a historical film that reworked this tradition and transformed it into almost neorealistic material. The film presented a completely desecrated image of the Middle Ages, of its castles, its dukes and its kings, ignorant adventurers without means, of these tournaments that were more like minor-league football matches played on a bad field in the outskirts.

– *Had you gathered a lot of documentation in preparation for the film?*

– Yes, we had done a lot of research. Nevertheless, I must say that there wasn't a lot of documentation available on this period. We set the film around the year 1000, more or less, of course. There weren't a lot of documents, there were the letters of Gregory the Great, fragments of paintings in Roman churches, very little in the way of iconography. So, the film is for the most part imaginary, made up; for example, the costumes, the sets. I must say Pietro Gherardi really contributed greatly to this; he understood immediately what I expected from him. I find the images we got extraordinary. We didn't have any precedent to go by; we made everything up, the characters, the psychology, the relationships between individuals, the places, the events, the language, everything was born out of nothing, without being able to refer to anything at all. This film's success – a tremendous success at least in Italy – was really due to the fact that we had presented an image of an epoch, one that was studied a lot in Italy, in a completely unconventional way. This was something I saw confirmed time and again in numerous debates I participated in, not only in Rome but also in many small provincial cities such as Arezzo or Lecce.

On the set of *Parenti serpenti*.

– *While preparing the film did you already have Vittorio Gassman in mind for the leading role?*

– Yes, the film was conceived with him in mind. Gassman perfectly represented this type of wandering knight, a bit narrow-minded and stupid, courageous, grandiloquent, adventurous. The film was also made for him because of his ability to express himself in that language based upon popular structures, old Italian, kitchen Latin. He knew how to express himself with grandiloquence in a language that all in all was very modest, very down-to-earth, he knew how to give it weight and this created a very funny contrast.

– *I know you like* Brancaleone alle crociate *less, though this film seems to me to be just as good as* L'armata Brancaleone.

– After having seen how successful the film was in Italy, the producer, Mario Cecchi Gori, immedia-

tely started hounding me the very next year to make a sequel. As for me, I really didn't want to, just as I never wanted to make any sequels. For many of my films – *Cops and Robbers, Big Deal on Madonna Street, The Great War* – the producer came to see me about putting together another adventure. I had always refused because in my opinion it's not good to, it can only express the exhaustion, the exploitation of an old idea: it really isn't something that appeals to me. I held my own for five or six years, then finally gave in when I thought I might be able to express different things; and, in fact, the movie is based on the Crusades. But in fact I shouldn't have accepted: *Brancaleone alle crociate* added nothing to *L'armata Brancaleone*. I'm convinced that the film should have remained unique. The second was less inspired, it was more structured, more polished, more conventional; the first was more open and also a little cruder, but that was the truth in it, too.

– *More recently,* Amici miei *has been a tremendous success in Italy as well as in France. To me it is an exceptional film in that it's a perfect blend of farce, derision and deep despair.*

– Pietro Germi had prepared the film and since I was very close to him, when illness kept him from shooting it, he asked me to take over for him. I got together with the screenwriters Pinelli, Benvenuti and De Bernardi to go over the script, not so much to change it as to reassess it; one thing in particular, we transferred the action from Bologna to Florence since I'm Tuscan and could feel the film better by setting it in a region I was familiar with. I liked the screenplay very much, especially because of the importance that death plays in it, an element which is much more pronounced than it might seem at first sight. It's a harsh story, without sentimentalism, that shows a very bitter humanity. Of course there is friendship, but even friendship only really serves to bring people together to have fun; it is never felt as a deep bond, it always remains something superficial. I liked this a lot because the Tuscan spirit basically is never sentimental; it consists of a certain cynicism, a certain skepticism. I like the film because it has that tone: old children who still continue playing games to ward off old age, death, so as not to be thrown into life, in order to ignore what's around them and to continue living a youth that no longer is. This seemed very hard to me and I think the film is very hard. I think that if *Amici miei* had such extraordinary success – which perhaps goes beyond the qualities in the film – it was really because of this element: behind the laughs and fun, the public got the feeling that there was a bitter sniggering that surpassed it all.

– This combining of laughs and despair is characteristic of Italian comedy.

– This is truly part of the Italian tradition; it's something that comes from the *commedia dell'arte.*

Commedia dell'arte heroes are always desperate poor devils who are battling against life, against the world, against hunger, misery, illness, violence. Nevertheless, all of this is transformed into laughter, transmuted into cruel joking, in mockery rather than wholehearted laughter. This approach belongs to a very Italian tradition that I have always defended: Italian comedy comes from this and it isn't true that it's vulgar, that it was always a matter of chamber pots, excrement, clysters, farts. Let's face it, there is a crude side, but this isn't important since the true underlying factor is the element of despair.

– That is where the deepest roots of Raffaele Viviani, of Totò, of Eduardo De Filippo and even Dario Fo can be found.

The horror of family reunions where conflicts, pettiness, financial rivalries might even lead to murder. Mario Monicelli's ***Parenti serpenti.***

– Certainly. In all the great comedians there is a rage inside that resolves itself in comedy, in mockery. This is indisputable; that's the way it is. This constitutes a foundation for Italian comedy. Naturally, we needed twenty, thirty years, to take stock of this essential characteristic.

– Drama and comedy are again brought together in A Very Little Man.

– In that film, even the first part that seems mainly comical is already very harsh, very unpleasant. Sordi's relationship with his colleagues in the office make us laugh but in reality it is an atmosphere that is perhaps even worse than what happens afterwards in the film. In my opinion, the first part is even more unbearable than the second where everything is explicit: someone is killed, the blood, death, those are things that we've seen before. However, the first part perhaps makes us laugh, but it is profoundly dramatic: the inhuman relationships with office colleagues, the department head, the absence of solidarity, the violence Sordi is constantly subjected to; family life, a wife who spends her life in the kitchen, Sordi who's a tyrant in the house...The nucleus of the film is there and so the tragedy in the second part develops quite naturally out of it.

– Speaking about this last film a little more, why did you have Sordi's son die in such an extremely quick and brutal way?

– It's something I wanted to do in that way. When the accident happens that morning when Sordi takes his son to the examination, I slowed everything down. The first part is very fast, then the morning of the examinations I slowed everything down, slower, slower, except for the moment of the theft and murder which is like lightning, since I wanted it to be like an accident that wasn't important to the film, something that just happens to occur. Because of this, anyone who talks, who discusses the film – the film has been very successful and people talk a lot about it – never remember that scene which, moreover, is fundamental. I'm glad it's like that since this is exactly what I wanted to achieve. No one ever thinks about this scene, so lightning quick it was. And then, this scene isn't the turning point of the film; in my opinion, the turning point occurs at another moment, when Sordi goes to the cemetery and enters that room with all the coffins piled up. That is the pivotal event of the film, from a stylistic point of view as well as in terms of the story's meaning. The accident, however, is just any accident; I didn't want to make it into anything of marked importance.

– Are there really rooms like that where coffins are piled up while waiting for a grave?

– Let's just say that things don't really happen the way I showed them in the film. Nevertheless, the

A recent photo of Mario Monicelli.

A scene from *Proibito*. At the center of the photo, seated, is Amedeo Nazzari.

problem does exist: you get a grave by paying certain people, by resorting to deals. So, there are rooms where coffins are kept; some have been left for years, others are visited by relatives since they're recent. Of course I exaggerated, I imagined a place with hundreds of coffins, with a crowd of people crying, carrying candles. In reality it exists, I simply transformed it, amplified it, but I didn't make it up.

– The problem brought up in the film caused a lot of fierce debate in Italy. Were you expecting this reaction?

– I'm very happy about this controversy. I made the film precisely because I wanted the hero to be a character the public could see themselves in: that's why I chose Alberto Sordi. For Italians, Sordi is a very popular figure, very likeable, much loved; I really wanted someone the public could identify with. I wanted the spectator, after seeing the film, to say: "Well no, I don't agree, I don't identify with him to the point of doing what he did." This was not always the case: some spectators identified with Sordi right up to the end: "Yes I would also have done the same thing." The debates arose out of these differences in points of view. I was quite pleased about this since this is what I was seeking. I didn't want to fool anyone; I wanted to show my hand. I wanted him to be a real character, a man, a man who loves his son even if his son isn't who the father believes he is. This mediocre man, whose son they kill, I wanted him to be just like that.

A scene from *La grande guerra/The Great War,* still today one of Monicelli's most famous films.

Confronted with this problem, which is a problem that really exists, the question of how to react arises: "What do I do? Do I kill in turn? Should I seek vengeance or not?" I wanted the public to feel this questioning. I didn't want an unpleasant father with a drug addict son: it would have been easy for me to create a character that the public would reject. I didn't want that, and chose an ambiguous process. As a result, controversy broke out in the press, on television; I was invited to participate in debates. Generally, after a while people left me on the side lines and they started discussing among themselves whether the father was right or not to have sought vengeance. Most often it is was the young who condemned the father's behaviour and the older people, instead, who found justifications for him: "You'll see, when you have children of your own; you'll change your minds." That was the most frequent argument.

– Discussions also broke out over how to interpret the mother's attitude when she was confronted with her son's murderer.

– This also deserved to be discussed. I wanted this scene's meaning to be open. Moreover, this opening came about as a result of certain factors without my

really even intending it myself. This is how it came about. Shelley Winters used the Strasberg method; she never wanted to know what would happen afterwards in the film; she used to say that the Strasberg method said that the actor should ignore the later developments in the story just as in life people never know what's going to happen to them next. So, they had killed her son and she thought she should hate the murderer. She never wanted to see the actor who played the part of the murderer. When we went to shoot the scene where she is brought by the side of her wounded son and she saw the actor I had chosen – I had purposely chosen a boy with an angelic face, à la Melozzo da Forlì; I wanted him to be fragile, even tender, just the opposite of what one would expect; someone very different from the son who on the contrary is mediocre, with a big nose, an actor who physically resembles Sordi a little – she asked me "How can I do it? With this actor I can't act the scene, he makes me feel tenderness, he makes me feel sorry for him." And I answered: "Act this scene the way you feel it, express your grief, show that he makes you feel sorry for him." And so there is a lot of ambiguity in this scene since we can't really tell if Shelley Winters hates the boy or feels pity for him.

– Did Alberto Sordi accept the character he was

playing as he was, or did he try to change him a little?

– Sordi tried to make the character a little closer to his own self. Sordi protected a certain image of himself that he wanted to present to the public; he had understood that I wanted to reverse this image, that I wanted the friendliness, the popularity, the public's favorable opinion of him, to be transformed into horror and disgust. On the one hand, he was aware that this was the film's point of view, on the other hand, unconsciously or consciously perhaps, I don't know, he defended his actor's image. Actors always want to be liked by their public, and all the more when it comes to an actor like Sordi, who has been admired for thirty years. So, he showed a little resistance in accepting to reverse this image. His attitude didn't bother me since this was also part of the film and the risk I had taken in choosing Sordi – if not, I would have chosen another actor. During the shooting, there was therefore this struggle going on, a somewhat open and friendly struggle: I was pulling from one side, and he was pulling from the other. The whole film went like that and I think the result is quite good; it made the film richer, since it gave birth to a lot of things and gave weight to scenes that we were shooting. Shelley Winters also had her own personal attitude on the set. Each one almost played their own real selves in the film.

– *Was the film's screenplay very different from the novel by Cerami?*

– The screenplay follows the novel by Vincenzo Cerami quite closely with, however, two changes: the first was the scene where Sordi takes his paralyzed wife to see the murderer, this scene wasn't in the book; the second was the ending. The sequence where Sordi is sitting in the little garden and where afterwards he has an argument with a young man and decides to follow him with his car – this wasn't in the book. The novel ends with the hero alone in his apartment and that's it. In the writing of the screenplay, Sergio Amidei helped me filter, give rhythm to the film. From a book, you always have to take out a lot of things and only leave the essential moments, you have to reassemble in one scene things that belong to three or four different ones. Amidei was very helpful in this.

– *In an interview you once said that you tried to make "national popular" films. In what sense did you use this expression which is one linked to the ideas of Gramsci?*

– I wanted to make films – for example, *The Great War, The Organizer,* and the two *Brancaleone* movies – that express the feelings, the problems, the truth of the people; films that are epics at the same time as being humble, small, everyday; films that represent the genuine and profound reality of the masses, the historical richness of the masses. When I made *The Great War,* there are two heroes who keep the film going, who make people laugh, but behind them there is an entire mass of people stirring. In the end, at least for us Italians, after the film is over, we have realized that these millions of soldiers who had gone to war were poor peasant farmers who didn't know how to read or write, who didn't know why they were fighting or against whom. In short, they didn't know anything. If I make a film on strikes, of course there's Mastroianni, however, at the end there is the deep truth of a people, a people that are present and must seek their affirmation by their own means.

I want to show that the small ordinary things in life are nevertheless important; it's a matter of finding the epic feeling in the little daily details of life, details that in fact represent great historic moments of a people. This was what I meant by national-popular film and I think that's what the expression "national-popular" means. In Italy we hardly ever make films of this kind, or rarely. As for me, I'd like to: I think it's what I know best how to do and I'd like to do it as often as possible. Unfortunately, it's very expensive... For example, I even wanted to make a film on the expedition of the "Thousand" and Garibaldi, from the angle I've just mentioned. This film was to have the kind of tone I'm fond of, the humorous and the grotesque, with a blend of the epic and the everyday; with this fervour and also with the ferment of these plebians, of these people with or without a clear understanding of the events they are involved in. And with the comings and goings of Garibaldi with his poncho in the midst of this populace looking at him without really knowing what it was all about. I would really have liked to have made that film, but from the looks of it, it seems very unlikely...

Ever present with his satirical eloquence when it comes to depicting changing mores, Dino Risi takes a look at a priest confronting celibacy and his fiancée (Sophia Loren). On the set of *La moglie del prete/The Priest's Wife*.

Dino Risi

– In the early days of your career, did you ever think that you would become a specialist of comedy?

– Everything happened on its own, in a way, almost without my realizing it, a bit like a painter who doesn't know what kind of artist he's going to be: he starts using colors, arranges them on the canvas and, little by little, he tries out various approaches and ends up with a certain style of painting. This is how I found my direction, too. Of course, a basic inclination is there, my natural sense of humor, taste for caricature, the fun I get observing people's tics – this has always filled me with curiosity. And then, too, the way I love stories: I'm attracted by the unfolding of events, to everything that happens, human relationships, people's behavior. All of this transformed everything I had inside of me into cinema, but it really wasn't a vocation, I ended up in cinema sort of by chance. I had discovered a type of work that I liked: apparently there was something I was succeeding in communicating to others and this was what made me continue.

– Lattuada studied architecture because he was forced to by his father, though all the while he had cinema on his mind. Was this also true for you and your medical studies?

– For me, too, it was a little because of my father's wishes, indirectly. My father was a doctor; he died when I was twelve. My brother and I were brought up by my mother, we both studied medicine, a little in memory of our father, as a homage to him. I wasn't thinking of cinema while I was studying, though I knew that I would never practice medicine. At one point I wanted to study psychiatry: I started specializing, but then became afraid of commiting myself to such a sad profession. My encounter with cinema was rather by chance: it was Lattuada who gave me a whiff of movie-making when he had me collaborate as assistant on Soldati's film *Old-Fashioned World,* for which he was the first assistant; and afterwards, when he

asked me to be his assistant on his own film, *Giacomo l'idealista.* Of course, I had discovered work that in fact really wasn't work at all, it was almost like a game. After the war, when I had graduated – my brother and I are both medical doctors – I decided not to become a doctor and took up journalism for about two years. Then I met a producer who made short subjects and started getting involved in cinema. It all came about quite easily.

– You participated especially in the development of an original genre, bittersweet comedy.

– By taking a look at Italian society, focusing on its foibles, drawing upon the "humors" it expressed, I ended up with this type of cinema which was already more or less in the air. There were other directors who had experimented in what was later called "Italian comedy." There had been Camerini in the thirties, a director who had already shown the same sensitivity and lightness in his way of representing the human situations of ordinary people. There had been Castellani with *Two Cents Worth of Hope,* a film that, in the thick of neorealism, represented a step forward. Castellani made fantasy-inspired neorealism that was later termed "pink neorealism." Thus I joined the ranks, not of militant realism, but of those films which later revealed themselves to be perhaps even more politically committed than the ones that claimed to be – in their stressing of the evils of Italian society; the evils that could also be shown in an amusing way.

– In the beginning, were you aware that you were confronting very serious subjects through comedy?

– Yes, of course, it was my eccentricity coming out. I felt this was a characteristic that could distinguish me from others, an expressive style, recognizable. Moreover, I immediately thought of using a special type of actor, the kind who came from theater comedy, from "variety," Tognazzi, Sordi, and then Gassman – a great theater player – whom I took on, and who little by little shifted over to the comedy of manners. Basically, it was with me in *The Easy Life* that he made his first comedy where he appeared as his natural self. Everyone feared that Gassman wasn't capable of being funny but, in fact, he was totally successful.

– *Can you define the Risi style?*

– I don't know, it's a rather hybrid style, a mixture. I've never condemned myself to one style, like some painters who always paint pears or bottles. I'm so curious that I find everything that happens around me interesting; this nature could have led me to make solely dramatic films. Critics like classifications, they always want to put you in a compartment – and watch out if you ever want to change. Billy Wilder, in America, is disturbing because he passes from one genre to another with equal ease. As for myself, I bring subjects to the screen that I'm interested in and which can be very dramatic, though I always add a pinch of irony in even the most serious stories.

– *Irony, and also sometimes cynicism?*

– In my opinion, cynicism isn't a defect, it isn't a negative attitude; it's a way of saying things as you try to get to the truth, without prejudices and without compromise. Cynicism is a very beautiful way of looking at reality, without pretending, without hiding anything.

– *In your approach to your stories you had a definite feeling of what was in the air, even a sort of intuition in terms of how Italy was evolving.*

– Yes, it's true. I've often made films that have anticipated problems to come. The film *In nome del popolo italiano* could have been made today, it perfectly represents the situation our country is living in right now: a judge who reveals all the catastrophes, all the corruption – the movie was really a premonition. And then there was *Mordi e fuggi* about terrorism, even before those terrible events occurred which shocked all of Italy. I could cite other films: I had this capacity to sense things that were in the air, which is important, I believe, for someone who wants to make comedies that reflect society.

– *You also showed great skill in recreating the "humors" of the past in films such as* The March on Rome *or* A Difficult Life.

– Those were historical films which, without apparently revealing great truths, without openly expressing an ideology in capital letters, captured the atmosphere of an epoch quite well: they spoke of the black and the white, the bitterness, and those curious and comical things to be found in the most dramatic situations. The Neapolitans say that there is no burial without a burst of laughter. Life is a mixture of the serious and the comical, the good and the bad, continuously.

– *Filmmaking isn't one creator's activity in the same way as painting or literature. Cinema is a collaborative art. Do you find this restricting?*

– On the contrary. I like collaborating with others in my work, even if I am by nature a solitary person. I never see anyone, I know very few people in the Italian movie world; I've never formed a group, I've always worked a little apart from others, isolated. Nevertheless, on the set I feel good in the midst of all the excitement, I become another person. My kind of sociability, apparently, makes me attracted to the feeling of adventure in cinema, the unpredictable side of things. I improvise a lot in my work, I'm not one of those directors who charge ahead with an iron-clad screenplay and all the shots planned beforehand. Instead, I believe in improvisation. Perhaps this is the quality which gives my films that natural touch which the public likes.

– *Comedy is a genre of elaborate cut-outs and rhythm.*

– I start with a definite plan: the film's outline is worked out very carefully. But afterwards, above all, I give it form during the shooting, like a painter at his canvas who adds various touches to give his painting the final colors. In short, I improvise on something that isn't improvised, something that is premeditated. Films that don't turn out well – often is because they lack preparation. This frequently happens in this profession where you often have to work in a hurry in order not to go over the budget. In cinema, a lot of things depend on money. At any rate, when a film wasn't working, I always realized it right away. A painter or writer can do as he pleases. With a piece of paper and a pencil, you can write the most beautiful novel in the world: the writer writes "war" and he doesn't need ten thousand extras in combat who cost a fortune.

– *How do you work with screenwriters? How much do you intervene at the writing stage?*

– Generally, I'm the author of the story. I entrust it to the screenwriters and let them work on it, inter-

Heiress to Gina Lollobrigida in her "Pane, amore" series, Sophia Loren, at the height of her splendor, seduces Antonio Cifariello in *Pane, amore e.../Scandal in Sorrento* by Dino Risi.

vening in the first phase, that is, during the treatment. Then I let them carry on, especially when I trust their work. For example, Age and Scarpelli often submitted screenplays that were perfect; and then, naturally, I come into play during the shooting. It's not out of laziness, but simply because I don't want to be bored with the film already, even before the first clap: if I know everything about the film I'm about to shoot, making it isn't fun anymore, or else, I get the impression that I've made it already. How many times have I been delighted that a film wasn't going to be made after all! The producers would tell me, "We don't have the money, we don't have a co-producer, no actors have been approached; we're going to cancel the shooting." But I was overjoyed, since it was a film that I had already worked out, and I really wanted to start thinking about the next one. I love novelty, I'm for adventure; even if in life I'm not an adventurous man, in cinema I am. I might add that I've never taken cinema too seriously, I'm not one of those furious cinephiles who live cinema like a great torture. Cinema is like life: we're in the hands of forces that are sometimes beyond our control.

– *In the way you plan your time, what place do you give to your work and your private life respectively?*

Vittorio Gassman and Jean-Louis Trintignant (with back turned) on the sunny road of an Italy basking in its economic boom. Dino Risi's *Il sorpasso/The Easy Life.*

– By "private life" I also mean just going for walks. I'm so very curious when it comes to observing other people's lives. I also like just doing nothing. My romantic life has been full of ups and downs, intense relationships that I've always tried to live with a bit of foolhardiness, always with a spirit of adventure; a taste for the unpredictable in human encounters. I'm sensitive to the fortunes of life, always curious about everything that happens.

– *Have you ever had any interferences between your private life and your work?*

– Rarely. I once made a film just to meet a woman. So it has happened, but generally a film has interested me enough so that I've put other things aside. Despite my anxious disposition there have practically never been interferences between my work and private life.

– *During the shooting of* Anima nera, *Gassman related that Rossellini some days didn't appear on the set because he was occupied with his love life. So, for him his private life was more important than the film?*

– Yes but Rossellini was an adventurer, he was a pirate on his corsair. He was always like that. In India, at one point he abandoned the troupe and the chief cameraman, Aldo Tonti, and left them stranded in the middle of the forest: he was in a Bombay hotel with Sonali Das Gupta and had completely forgotten about the film. There was also the love affair with Ingrid Bergman and all the others. But Rossellini was a fascinating figure, he had that force, that capacity to work fast and well. He had a particular kind of genius, something that wasn't programmed. He lived from day to day; we should also remember that these were the postwar years, a time when movie-making was more adventurous, more improvised. Probably when he neglected a shooting it was because the film didn't interest him. When he made *Open City, Paisan* or *Germany, Year Zero*, he stayed glued to the camera. *Anima nera* was probably a film that he really didn't like very much; in fact, it wasn't at all successful.

– *And your relationship with your sons?*

– My relationship with my sons is very beautiful, I took care of them a lot until they were ten, twelve years old; then, I felt they were old enough and could manage without me and could live with their mother. I also took less care of them because I was working a lot, I was shooting a film a year, I was away a lot. We grew closer again later, we love each other very much and see each other often. Marco has made two or three films, *Mery per sempre, Ragazzi fuori, Il muro di gomma,* which were successful, and Claudio, too, made a beautiful film, *Pugni di rabbia,* about amateur boxers, that unfortunately was not a success. Today, all you have to do is make one film that isn't successful and you risk not making any films for a long time. He plans to make a second film produced by Marco who has set up a production company called Sorpasso Film – a homage to his father...

– *Does it seem that a certain spontaneous way of moviemaking has been lost?*

– We should make cinema the way it was born, when we first held this toy in our hands. We turned the crank and saw reality, with a few corrections, which is normal: everyone sees reality through his own eyes. But I don't think you should torture yourself over a film as certain directors do today who always want to make a masterpiece: there's nothing worse than forcing yourself to produce a masterpiece; it's enough to ruin a film.

– *You've worked mainly with great actors, rarely with amateurs, people off the street as in the days of neorealism.*

– For small roles I might take amateurs: a person has a handsome face, I might have him say a few lines. But in general I use professional actors. Certain great Italian actors have remained unspoilt by the profession. For example, Tognazzi is an actor who seems to come right off the street, the same with Sordi. Their force is in their ability to express themselves naturally, while at the same time being professionals. With others, we get a stronger feeling of craft, for example, Manfredi. Another natural actor is Mastroianni, a very pleasing actor who is always successful because he is "the man next

Top: The derisory days of two half-wits recruited into the Fascist "squads" to capture Rome. Ugo Tognazzi and Vittorio Gassman in Dino Risi's *La marcia su Roma/ The March on Rome.*

Left: A scathing portrait of an amoral society, Ugo Tognazzi in the episode "Il povero soldato" in Dino Risi's *I mostri/Opiate '67.*

Opposite right: Why not betray your wife if all she does is stay on the telephone all the time? Nino Manfredi and Virna Lisi in Dino Risi's episode "La telefonata" from the film *Le bambole/The Dolls.*

door," the man off the street. Even an actor like Gassman who comes from the theater – one of those who learns scripts by heart and remembers all the lines – evolved. As a great professional, little by little, he understood cinema, he realized that the screen actor shouldn't give the impression that he's acting but has to be natural. In fact, as he grew older, he became better and better, he gave up certain excesses, certain ways of emphasizing, certain efforts to try to make people understand the underlying intentions of what he was doing. If an actor has a good face and his face is right and he resembles the character, he must absolutely not add anything more, since even pain can be expressed in one look, without shouting. This is the way it has to be done in cinema, whereas in theater you have to make yourself heard in the last row of the stalls and right up to the gallery.

– You've only spoken about actors, what about your work with actresses?

– I've spoken of actors because I've usually always made masculine cinema, a cinema of actors. Of course, I've also directed actresses and developed a good rapport with some of them. The female roles in my films, the films that I've made, it's true, have always been a little "on the side."

Top: Vittorio Gassman in drag with Salvatore Borgese in "The Muse" episode of *I mostri/Opiate '67.*

Left: A 'recital' of characters and situations for a quick-change actor at the peak of his art; Nino Manfredi in the episode "Vedo nudo" from Dino Risi's *Vedo nudo.*

The young generation on the move: Luca Venantini, Anna Falchi and Edoardo Scatà in *Giovani e belli*.

– Could you explain what you mean by making "masculine cinema" in more detail?

– I had these four actors whom I worked a lot with, Sordi, Gassman, Tognazzi, Manfredi and also Mastroianni, these five actors. The first four appeared in almost all my films and so the stories centered around male characters. They were the heroes. Women were always slightly in the background. These were actors whom – especially Gassman who was in fifteen of my films – I had a good rapport with. It was the pleasure of working with friends, not actors: we understood each other in just one glance, without long explanations. We had a relationship of trust and esteem: on the set everything always went very well.

– You're together for the length of a film and then everyone goes his own way. It's an intermittent friendship...

– This is also part of what's beautiful about filmmaking, this continual voyage, this perpetual change of places, of people... You're together for the duration of the shooting; it's like on a train, at the end you get off, say good-bye, you say "we'll call each other" and then you never do, "we'll have dinner one night" but that dinner never happens...

The material misery and moral distress of the *borgate* of Rome. Ettore Scola directs a group of children in *Brutti, sporchi e cattivi/Down and Dirty*.

Ettore Scola

(FIRST INTERVIEW)

– *You have often given Rome an important place in your films.* The Motive Was Jealousy *in 1970 offers us an image of the Eternal City. How did your rapport with this city develop?*

– Even if I often make films locked up in interiors, the city has always been strongly bound to my themes. One of my first cinematographic memories was on Piazza Vittorio where I lived – today my mother lives in that apartment – a working-class neighborhood of Rome. It was the biggest square in the city, three or four times vaster than Piazza del Popolo or Piazza Mazzini. In the middle there was a garden with Roman ruins and then, around it, the stalls of the biggest market in Rome. There were arcades around this square since it was in the 'Umbertino' area of Rome, whose architecture was attributed to Umberto I in 1902-1903. There are two 'Umbertino' neighborhoods in Rome: the one around Piazza Vittorio and the Esquilino; and the one in Prati where my last film was set, *The Family.* Prati is a good bourgeois neighborhood, middle and upper middle class, of professors, well-off shopkeepers, small-scale property owners. Piazza Vittorio, on the other hand, was a very working-class neighborhood. So, one morning, on my way to school – we used to walk to school, something almost no one does today – I was crossing the Piazza Vittorio to go to the Umberto I high school, which was next to the Santa Maria Maggiore basilica, and I saw an incredible sight: the square was militarily occupied by some strange troops; it had been taken over by strange weapons, projectors and huge lights, trucks, cars. I didn't go to school and stayed there to watch: I saw Vittorio De Sica filming *The Bicycle Thief,* the scene at dawn when the sweepers meet and set out to find the bicycle. Lamberto Maggiorani, Gino Saltamerenda, a character actor famous for his corpulent physique, were all there. I don't know if that was when my love for cinema was born – I was seventeen years old – but that day I felt like I had been struck by lightning. Without resorting to simplistic psychoanalytical explanations, for me, the cinema and the square, the cinema and

The patriarch of the *borgate:* Nino Manfredi in a grandiose portrayal. Ettore Scola's *Brutti, sporchi e cattivi/Down and Dirty.* On his left, Linda Moretti; on his right, Maria Luisa Santella: his wife and his lover.

Rome, were born together; and this might explain my affection for this neighborhood, for Piazza Vittorio where I pass by everyday to see my mother; my affection for De Sica and my admiration for *The Bicycle Thief* – one of my most beloved films.

In my films, the city is always present since the kind of cinema I make, which I certainly didn't invent, is one that represents other things than solely my interior poetic world, one that doesn't abandon itself to my imaginative fantasies. Federico Fellini, on the contrary, can, or better still, *must* do without Rome as it really exists: he recreates Rome himself and the one he creates in the studio is sometimes more real than the real city itself. The Rome he has rebuilt is very beautiful, the squares, the restaurants... The sea at Fregene that he reconstructed closed up in studio 5 at Cinecittà was part of his distorted reality. As for me, I don't have this kind of inspiration; my inspiration, let's say, is more neorealist, more in direct contact with life and with reality, and therefore with the city. I would hesitate to build a square, a street, in the studio; I wouldn't recognize them anymore. I need trees, sky, real life, real passers-by, everything that can truly happen at a given moment. In this respect, I believe the city is very present and very important in my films.

– In your films you sometimes use famous places in Rome and sometimes settings that are not very well known. Do you scout around a lot for locations before you start shooting?

– The phase of finding locations, looking around for the places where I want to shoot, is just as important as the screenplay to me. Sometimes, while I'm still in the process of writing, my steady set designer Luciano Ricceri and I already start looking around for locations. For example, in my next film, *Captain Fracassa's Journey*, though the screenplay hasn't been written yet and we only have a treatment, we've already been to France looking for locations, we've already found several places where we'll shoot. I write screenplays with my settings in mind. I therefore follow a reverse process than what is usually considered normal, that is, first of all the writing and then the choice of locations. The search for locations

is very important, just as important as writing the dialogues or the casting.

For the settings, it all depends on the story you want to tell. In fact, I don't like to always show the same sides of Rome. Rome has its greatness as any metropolis, Paris or London; it has that quality of getting different cities to co-exist in the same space. In Rome, you can identify neighborhoods that are Naples, Milan or Turin. The emigrants from the South have brought their traditions, their culture; and the city, as it has grown, has absorbed this presence and adopted different physiognomies. Around the historical center, which is Rome, neighborhoods have been built that resemble the home cities of their inhabitants. In certain squares in Rome, you really get the impression you're in the south of Italy, in Sicily or Calabria: the people have built the city after the image of their habits, their customs, their traditions. So, when I shot *Down and Dirty,* it never occurred to me to invent a shanty town built in a studio, I looked around among the shanty towns that really existed. In *We All Loved Each Other So Much,* I needed a place where three friendships come to an end. I went to the rather melancholic Trieste quarter, a good place for an atmosphere of farewells, one that gives an impression of solitude. I don't know if you remember that scene, shot from above, with a man drawing the Virgin Mary on the ground and the three heroes each going their own ways, taking three different streets. I filmed that scene on Piazza Caprera in the Trieste quarter. So, truly, the city is never just a simple backdrop; it is part of the atmosphere and the conception itself of a scene.

– You have rarely filmed in the country. What does the city represent for you; is it a concentration of individuals and subjects to treat?

– I should first of all confess my insensitivity to "pretty panoramas." Certain colleagues of mine have said to me: "There's a beautiful seascape with palm trees, bays and crystal waters in the Seychelles or even Sardinia." I just can't feel that kind of fascination. It's a little like sports, another one of my shortcomings. I just can't, even if I wanted to rationally, get interested in football. I even went to the stadium,

just as a matter of study; I couldn't wait until it was over. Perhaps it's a culture you have to acquire when you're very young, I don't know. In the same way, as a child, I never went on vacation: we stayed at Piazza Vittorio all summer. The city became more beautiful, it was even more mine. Colle Oppio was the garden of my childhood, of my adolescence, of my first flirts. I went from games to kisses at Colle Oppio: it was my Seychelles, my Sardinia... A beautiful natural wonder doesn't inspire me; however, the city, even at its ugliest, inspires me. In *The Motive Was Jealousy,* I showed a crumbling, devastated Rome: there were certain feelings that could be expressed in a poetic way on the debris, the gravel, the plastic bags filled with sweepings, amidst the industrial refuse and garbage. This is also Rome; it's a big city that shelters all kinds of men and women, feelings and problems. What interests me more than anything are the people, the faces. I think that the city expresses these stories much more than beautiful country landscapes or great mountain tops.

– In Trevico Torino: Viaggio nel Fiat-Nam, *in 1973, you used the city of Turin to depict a hostile place, a place unadapted to human life.*

– Here again, I don't think the film could have existed in any another city other than Turin. The hero was the city, the way of life in that city. Turin is an Italian city symbol: a mistaken governmental policy gave impetus to automobiles when basic needs had not been satisfied. Highways were built before hospitals; big racing tracks for cars were built before schools. This weird policy led to the so-called "economic boom," which, in fact, was a boom for very few people and a crash for the majority. Turin became a racist city and a city of victims. This convergence of contradictory situations, human frictions, could only lead to a confrontation. It was decided to bring workers from all over Italy to work at the Fiat factory there, but Fiat hadn't foreseen any housing, no company cafeterias for these people, absolutely nothing. Everything was left up to the personal initiative of these new arrivals, the recipients of this great gift: a job. Work was certainly not a right, it was a gift granted to a few elect, and then these elect had to manage on their own and confront the problems of living in the city. In *Trevico Torino: Viaggio nel Fiat-Nam,* the presence of Turin is therefore very important. Of course, it wasn't a city I regarded with the same affection as Rome. Rome is very special: beneath the apparent

All the enthusiasm of a Mediterranean filmmaker directing his actors. Ettore Scola on the set of *Maccheroni/Macaroni;* seated nearby, Marcello Mastroianni.

hostility of the city, Rome has this ability that other cities don't, to welcome everyone. Perhaps the hostility of Turin towards the emigrants would never have occurred in Rome, even in a similar political and social situation.

– Vorrei che volo, *shot in 1980, returns to the problems of the city of Turin.*

– *Vorrei che volo* is a little like a sequel to *Trevico Torino:* instead of the worker, there's the worker's son. The worker in *Trevico Torino* moves to Turin, he eventually finds a job and lives a life of misery. He lives under the roof, squeezed into one single room with all of his family. His children carry two worlds within them, the North and South; even in their language, they mix words from the South and words from Turin. There is, therefore, a deep split

within them. One of these children shows this split by stealing: he steals to express an instinctive aggression against what he feels is a hostile society. I went to a prison for minors, a prison for children, a kind of big nursery kept by warders. I chose a child about eight or nine years old, imprisoned for theft and, under my responsibility, I signed a discharge for the director who entrusted him to me for a few days. I sent this child out on a spree, notifying the people who eventually might be robbed that they would be reimbursed; and the boy, followed constantly by the camera, took us everywhere. He knew where you could best rob, he knew which markets were the most confused and disorderly, the most crowded trams. The child then proceeded to rob several people, helping us to penetrate into the various realities of the city, in various neighborhoods. At the time, Diego Novelli was mayor of Turin – Diego

Novelli had written the screenplay for *Trevico Torino* with me, and afterwards became mayor of Turin, not thanks to the film but thanks to his personal merits – a great Communist mayor who did a lot for the the people of the South and who succeeded in curbing certain blights on society. In *Vorrei che volo* I also showed that this city was in the process of changing, and the film ends on a note of hope for the child.

– You're now working on a film project about Rome. What's it about?

– I can't define it very clearly. It won't be a fiction film and it won't be a documentary either: I can't always remain as detached and objective as someone who makes documentaries should be. It will therefore be a composite formula in which the documentary, the general interest news item, but definitely also fiction, will come into play, fiction that won't be acted by professional actors but played by people who live in the city, as for example what I did in *Trevico Torino* or *Vorrei che volo*. I'll have these stories of solitude, work, love, acted by those who live them day in and day out. It's a portrait of Rome made with love and so, to preserve this love, I shouldn't start off by having already defined and precise plans. A woman who is loved, I think you have to love her just the way she is, without the presumptuousness of changing her, without wanting to do her hair, to make her up, to dress her differently. Rome is this very beautiful woman full of defects, full of bones, very crude, very brusque, apparently hostile and yet full of tenderness. I hope I'll succeed in doing this portrait. Of course, it won't be exhaustive since I don't think it would ever be possible to define Rome. Nevertheless, it will

be a sincere, direct portrait. I don't know what the result will be, I don't know what genre of film I'm going to end up with, I'll know once it's finished.

– How was the idea for this film born?

– A desire... When I've made other films, when I've filmed in the streets of Rome, I've always been curious about this city. I'm much more intrigued by this city than any other that I may visit as a tourist. Of course I'm fascinated by Paris, by the city's coherence, by its proud self-confidence. Rome, however, is a city that destroys itself, isn't proud of itself, of its past. Rome is vanishing day after day,

Naples liberated by the Allies: in the sublime gardens of the cloister of Santa Chiara, an American soldier and a beautiful young Neapolitan woman make a couple full of promise for a souvenir photo. Jack Lemmon in *Maccheroni/Macaroni* by Ettore Scola.

The triumph of intimist cinema through its use of the ordinary to express the torments of contemporary Italy's history: Monica Scattini, Athina Cenci, Alessandra Panelli, the three sisters in Ettore Scola's *La famiglia/The Family.*

spends itself at every street corner. This attitude strongly excites my curiosity. Perhaps because I was born here, I know how to go out in search of Rome. I wouldn't know about Paris. If it were Paris, I would probably make an oleographic portrait, beautiful, full of admiration, but without hate. For Rome, there is also hate; I think you also need this feeling to draw a good portrait.

– *What do you think about real estate speculation, a problem you dealt with in* We All Loved Each Other So Much?

– In that film, and also in others. Rome has a strange destiny, it's a city just for passing though, and a city for sacking, from the Barbarians right up to the Caltagirone family – those builders who were even sent to prison – from pontifical troops to French troops, the American army to armies of building constructors who have occupied Rome in the bloodiest way possible and whose destruction is even worse than any of the bombers ever were. For centuries and centuries, Rome's destiny has been to be sacked and to oppose in its depths a majestic resistance against all: they've all been here, Attila and all the rest, nevertheless they've "passed through" and behind them, Rome has remained; of course, every time a little more slashed up, every time a little more covered in scars, like a woman always a little uglier, though nevertheless no less great...

– *In this perspective, we think of the buildings of the Fascist era, for example, the huge building in* A Special Day *or the EUR district.*

– It's like wrinkles: some women with the passing

of time become more beautiful, wrinkles are part of their charm. I remember all the suspicion, all the hatred, all the bitterness and also all the humor which EUR caused. However, nowadays, when you happen to pass through EUR, the mixture of classicism and functionalism, in a district that moreover doesn't function anyway, since nothing works in Rome, it has a certain charm. I don't feel that EUR's classical form clashes with the rest of the city: it's another face of Rome that is also appropriate. The same goes for some buildings that seemed ugly, for example, the monument to Vittorio Emanuele, the "typewriter," the "wedding cake," for a reception. Of course, habit comes into play, but anyway, Piazza Venezia, if there hadn't been this horrible monument, would now be the site of fifty-story buildings: so it's better to have this monument. In all cities, for example in Paris with its Eiffel Tower, we find structures that aren't beautiful, that are irrational or aesthetically questionable edifices. Nevertheless, with the passing of time, they become part of the physiognomy of the city.

(SECOND INTERVIEW)

– *Before becoming a film,* Le Bal *was a show created by the Théâtre du Campagnol troupe. How did the passing from stage to screen happen?*

– I had seen the show in 1981 and had really liked it a lot, just as I had seen it, as a spectator; I wasn't thinking in terms of a film. And then, over a meal with Gilles Sandier, who had seen *Le Bal* seven or eight times, Gilles said to me, "It would be a great film for you." As for me, I really hadn't given it much thought since I think that at the time there was already a vague project

to make a French film based on *Le Bal*. However, a little while later, the producer Giorgio Silvagni asked me to think about the project. I took a little while to answer – I'm a little long when it comes to deciding things, and then I still had to make *La nuit de Varennes* – but I saw that it was a show that was strangely close to me, close to the Italian style in many respects. It was a little like Italian-style comedy, that is, an indirect way of looking at history, of important events in life through an ordinary man, the usual everyday character to shadow, with his little mannerisms, his little hopes, his little encounters, his troubles. I liked it. I didn't have any big problems getting into the spirit of the show; it was even an idea I could have had myself or that the screenwriters Furio Scarpelli or Ruggero Maccari could have come up with. It was something familiar, I got into it right away. And then, we did a good adaptation with Scarpelli and Maccari as well as with Jean-Claude Penchenat, who came to Rome often, whom we kept informed of what we were doing. We enlarged the outline of the stage show. From this structure, we worked the various periods slightly more scientifically, with a less impressionistic tone.

Ettore Scola, attentive, on the set of *Splendor*.

The story of a troupe of Italian players on their way to Paris. Massimo Troisi, Ornella Muti, Massimo Wertmüller, Toni Ucci, Lauretta Masiero, Tosca D'Aquino, Emmanuelle Béart in Ettore Scola's *Il viaggio di Capitan Fracassa/Captain Fracassa's Journey.*

– In the stage version, Le Bal *began at the time of Liberation. In the film it began in 1936. Why this shifting back in time?*

– Biologically, I saw no reason why a film made by a fifty-two-year-old man should begin in the forties. Why not begin from childhood, from the thirties, which was precisely the Fascist period in Italy and the experience of the Front populaire in France. Even if in Italy there hadn't been a Front populaire, anti-fascist sentiment did exist. It also seemed to us that to cover a span of fifty years – this ballroom that lives through fifty years – led to something more complete, more rounded off. The stage show had other centers of interest; in addition to Liberation and today, certain very spiritual moments like the dance organized by the workers' company. Nevertheless, it still was somewhat the repetition of the analysis of certain particular milieux. This suggested another kind of structure: we

could imagine setting everything in the present, a contemporaneousness, in choosing ten different milieux, ten different ways of meeting, dancing, with company workers, on the terrace with intellectuals... As there was this historical indication that interested me a lot, it was useless to set more things in the present, one was enough. Moreover, I had never liked the ending of the stage show. It was a little desperate, a message about incommunicability that I found a little dated: these people who couldn't dance, who crossed each other without meeting, one screaming, the other tearing clothes. That character with an overly programmed pessimism; with our society in crisis, we have no choice but to be pessimistic. Nevertheless, I am still optimistic about hope: these people come to dance to try to change, to meet someone, to escape their gray lives. Even if that particular evening nothing happens, even if they leave just the way they came in, alone, isolated, this doesn't mean that they won't come back again the next Saturday. Basically, man is stronger than all wars, than all the events that can occur and go by. Man remains, always.

– At the end of Le Bal, *despite the concern for avoiding an "overly programmed pessimism" it seems to me that the dominant tone remains one of despair.*

– I would have felt like a liar if I had ended the film on a triumphalist note, a happy ending with dancers going home in couples: they've found their companion, company, they've resolved their existential problem! It's not so easy. The crisis is there, and the crisis of man in this second half of the century is serious; it questions values, all existing political systems, capitalist, socialist. We are in a period of mutation and it would be a little simplistic to deny that problems exist, or not to solve them. The ending is therefore a moment of despair, but it is also a moment of hope. It was honest, realistic, not to have made it into something happy. Things are like that: we are living a time of difficulties in our relationships with others, we can't solve our problems in one afternoon. For me, it was therefore right that they should go home alone, just the way they had come, with even one disillusion more. That particular Saturday they were disillusioned.

Nevertheless, the week after, they would come back looking for a new disillusion, but they would come back... The basic needs of man – to affirm his own vitality, his own dignity, his own right to a rapport with another, whether it be love, friendship, dialogue – will survive forever.

– When you were thinking about making Le Bal,

Concentrating, Ettore Scola on the set of *Il Viaggio di Capitan Fracassa/Captain Fracassa's Journey* with Claudio Amendola, Massimo Troisi, seated – brilliant Punchinello – and Massimo Wertmüller.

did you decide immediately to keep the Théâtre du Campagnol troupe?

– Yes, I decided to, right away, and I never had any doubts about it, even if sometimes people advised me, as you can imagine, to take Mastroianni for one role or Trintignant for another. First of all, I liked the Théâtre du Campagnol actors very much, I had liked their way of acting. I think that the principal value of the play was in the performance of the actors. And then, can we really speak of actors? For me they weren't actors, they weren't mimes, they were something different, they were real individuals who were offering things to the public that the spectators already knew. So they weren't really actors who created, made things up. And then, I don't know whether well-known faces would have been as effective at evoking the people they were supposed to. I get the impression that in the film we see thousands of people, even if they're always the same twenty actors. Each one has behind him, all in a line, a million people, all the same. The actor is more his own real self: Mastroianni is Mastroianni; however, each character in *Le Bal* is a category of humanity, the shy man, the vulgar man, the authoritarian man, the idiotic man, the shy woman, the audacious woman...

– *Apart from a few changes in make up and costumes, the actors play fifty years of the lives of their characters practically without any changes of physiognomy. Why did you choose to do this, when it was so easy in movies to make actors appear younger or older?*

– I asked myself that question in one or two instances: maybe for the credibility of a first meeting that had taken place fifty years before – they would have been sixteen at the time – mightn't it be necessary to have younger actors? So, the problem did come up. I think I solved it, not by ignoring

A scene from *Le Bal*.

it, but on the contrary by stressing it: they were always themselves, always the same. Besides a few wigs, a few light rejuvenating strokes, I left them just as they really were. They had a representative function, they symbolized human patterns, social categories, there was therefore no physical element, no indication of age, of civil status. In addition, young people had never frequented this kind of ballroom. The young had always gone to other places – dances for young people – and today, to discos. The ballroom in the film was always the place for people who were a little more lonely, a little more miserable, sexually and sentimentally, people who were searching for something there. So I really didn't need very young actors.

– *You added a few Italian actors who weren't in the stage show.*

– Yes, I added a café waiter who grows old with the ballroom. This is the only human element that, like the objects, goes through all the periods. I also added the toilets, and from there came the need for a toilet attendant. The toilets are a little like the backstage of the ballroom, the background. They are important: they are the place where you go to check your own irresistibility, certain things happen there. If I hadn't had problems of the film's length, I would even have included more scenes in the toilets, I would have studied the behavior of the men and the women alone in the toilets. Finally, I added the character of the woman who never dances. Certain women, who knows why, are wallflowers. They aren't necessarily ugly, but that's just the way it is, they have the nature of someone who is never invited to dance. So those were the three Italian performers I added; I didn't add them just because it was a co-production, but rather because I thought they represented three elements that were missing in the stage version.

– *In terms of the characters' nationalities, the café waiter was the only Italian.*

– That character was Toni de Renoir, he was a little

Italian emigré, he had fled Italy in 1934 or 1935 because of Fascism. He got to Paris, he found a little job, he became a waiter in a ballroom where there was a boss with a thick moustache, gruff but good-hearted. And so he stayed there, in that ballroom, he became more urban, more French, he lived with the portraits of his mother and of Garibaldi. He was an Italian who was just there, perhaps in a way he was me a little. I don't know. There was an old record he had brought with him and, during the war, he listened to De Sica singing *Parlami d'amore Mariù,* a very popular song in Italy that De Sica had sung in Mario Camerini's *Gli uomini che mascalzoni.* In France this song became *Le chaland qui passe. J'attendrai* is also an Italian song, it's *Tornerai* by maestro Olivieri. I think that a common musical heritage was shared between France and Italy. After the war, the Americans immediately arrived on the scene; a music from elsewhere started taking over Europe. I remember during the war, I was ten, a friend had a record by Louis Armstrong. When we listened to it, it was truly the American Dream as we imagined it. America represented freedom. Over there, everything was in advance. So there was this great admiration for America and I think that the disillusionment was all the greater the admiration being so tremendous. America has always paid for this: to have been so greatly admired, to have represented so many things during the war: rescue, power, the struggle against the Germans. The American troops were coming... Everything was glorious, desirable. And then, little by little, we began feeling colonized, oppressed. The Americans themselves felt this disillusionment. If we speak, for example, to Americans in our profession, we realize that they are ill at ease to be American, though in the past they had had a feeling of supremacy over others. The American intellectual hasn't felt good about himself since the Vietnam War, just as the Soviet intellectual can't feel very comfortable either, it's all so inconvenient. Sometimes there are advantages being from a small country.

Francesco Rosi calls the set of *C'era una volta/More than a Miracle* to attention.

Francesco Rosi

(FIRST INTERVIEW)

– *Your first film,* The Challenge, *was set in Naples. How was it that you immediately felt the need to make a film in your hometown?*

– The story I told in *The Challenge* appeared in the 'news in brief' column and involved the covered markets of Palermo and Catania. Originally, since it originated in this kind of issue, I had set the film in Sicily. Afterwards I changed it geographically when a very famous crime occurred involving the covered market trafficking in Naples. So at that point I decided to set the film in Naples: it seemed truer that way and gave me the opportunity of bringing a city to the screen that was really part of me. By combining the life of a city and the trafficking that have developed there in one story, by revealing the tacit agreements between the various powers – official power and unofficial power, legal power and criminal power – I could present an image that corresponded to actual reality. Don't forget that I made this film in 1957 and that none of the filmmakers who had dealt with Naples up to then had ever managed to break out of clichés in the way they depicted the city. My intention was precisely to reveal the more hidden side of the city.

– *In 1963 with* Hands Over the City, *you give an even more complete picture of Naples.*

– The problem of real estate speculation exists in all cities. I felt that by finding a way to reveal both the apparent life of a city and the hidden life of that same city, it was possible to show not only Naples, but also the entire world: real estate speculation is one of the most widespread of evils. And, in fact, *Hands Over the City* immediately had many repercussions; perhaps even more abroad than in Italy. I adopted the point of view of a citizen who was try-

Francesco Rosi, the filmmaker as social crusader.

ing to understand the reason for the city's transformation, a transformation not so much of the face of the city, but of its soul. This was the kind of city younger generations are growing up in. We shouldn't be surprised if the reservoir of delinquency is filling up with adolescents and young people. It's easy for this reservoir to find individuals whose resources are just waiting to be exploited.

Cities have been transformed into inhuman places; no one has worried about giving younger generations the possibility of establishing a good rapport with nature, with work, with leisure. They've expanded in a chaotic way, in terms of nothing but speculative criteria and with no thought to man. I felt that these themes might be of interest to spectators as citizens, not as spectators just going to see a movie. And also, at the same time, that this film could be like an x-ray of Naples, the city I knew best since it was the city of my childhood, of my adolescence, of the first experiences of my youth.

Naturally, the details had to be shown in the most rational, the most lucid way possible and also in such a way as to express emotion, so that spectators would become involved in this investigation of a city. My worry was that the situation might be represented in too simplistic a manner. The film's basic story corresponded to this need for rational expression: the purchase price of a square meter of land in the city outskirts increases incredibly – in *Hands Over the City* the increase of 5000% is cited, which is a percentage that corresponded very well to reality – if you managed to bring public utilities, electricity, gas, sewage, public transport, the telephone, etc., to this square meter of land. Of course, if these services were installed at the expense of the community, the profit was net for the owner; the 5000% went entirely into the pockets of those who had organized the project. So I had to show how public services, that is, this wealth that belongs to the community, was brought to privately owned land, to land that was later resold at astronomical prices by speculators.

As I said before, I was putting myself in the position of the citizen trying to understand what was happening: at one point, tacit agreements between economic powers and low politics become evident, it's easy to see the corruption of certain characters, corruption that concerns the life of the city and has tragic consequences for citizens unaware of this kind of trafficking. The way the city functions is almost entirely revealed during the Naples municipal council sessions, with the debate between political forces and economic powers. I showed the different kinds of impact criminal forces could have when economic power and low politics joined forces in the pursuit of unlawful objectives.

In the poorer quarters of Naples where the *camorra* recruits its dealers and hired men. José Suarez and Nino Vingelli in Francesco Rosi's *La sfida/The Challenge.*

– *It was with a mixture of rage and reason that you revealed certain political workings.*

– This more or less characterizes a lot of my films – by giving all the space needed to emotions and feelings, and at the same time not losing control over rationality and ideas. This is the aspiration of all Neapolitans a little: the conflict between the harmony of reason and the fantasy of passion, of feelings; this is somewhat the dialectic that makes up the Neapolitan soul.

– *There is a return to Naples in* Lucky Luciano, *in* Illustrious Corpses – *even if here it's a metaphorical city – and, finally, in* Three Brothers. *Unlike your first films, a new problem emerges: drugs.*

– I started dealing with the problem of drugs in *Lucky Luciano*. The problem is brought up when drugs replace all previously existing criminal activities. Compared to drug trafficking, all other rackets become less profitable. Lucky Luciano anticipated all of these problems, a kind of warning, an alarm. It was common knowledge that the network necessary to create, develop and spread drug trafficking on an international basis needed sorting areas located in the heart of the Mediterranean, like Sicily. But these were things that took time: focusing on this problem through the character of Lucky Luciano – with the myth of the retired gangster – offered possibilities for discussion, analysis, of a problem that many already foresaw as the real threat of the future. My collaborators and I did nothing but gather documents, information on things that people already knew. However, this information had to be brought out into the open with a film that wouldn't be the usual gangster movie, but a film that highlighted a threat that could represent – and I was later proven right – the real problem of the years to come. Indeed the spreading of drugs in Italy, the trafficking between Italy and the other countries of Europe, and even the United States, has now become the most profitable criminal activity of all others, the most serious continuous threat to younger generations. Up to twenty years ago, Italy had been immune to this calamity. *Lucky Luciano,* a film now fifteen years old, picked up the first signs of a transformation that would later erupt violently.

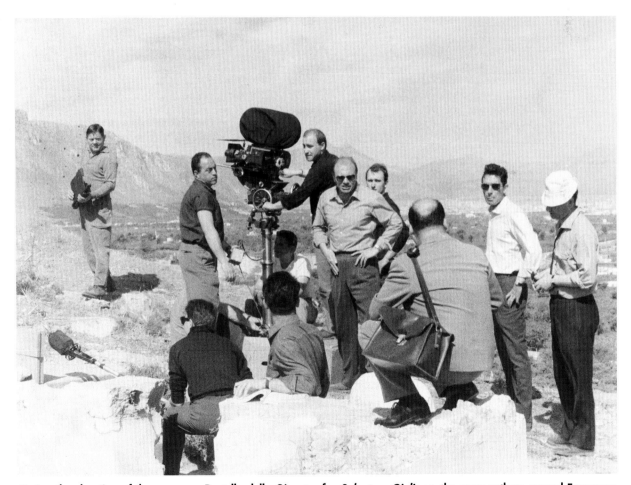

During the shooting of the sequence Portella della Ginestra for *Salvatore Giuliano,* the crew gathers around Francesco Rosi (with dark glasses in the center). At the camera, Pasqualino De Santis and on the right, with dark glasses, chief cameraman Gianni Di Venanzo.

– In Hands Over the City *you show the collusion between real estate speculators and politicians. Do you think a similar collusion exists between politicians and drug traffickers?*

– I can't answer that with certainty. Nevertheless, we are led to suspect that tacit agreements do exist: I don't think that such huge interests can be limited only to the world of crime. All you have to do is remember that, as shown in *Lucky Luciano,* the drug problem is a topic under debate in New York, at the United Nations headquarters. All you have to do is keep in mind that the first drug trafficking in Italy used the channels of a pharmaceutical manufacturer, the company Schiapparelli! From these signs we can very easily imagine that the spreading of drugs world-wide is not only limited to the specialized channels of organized crime. It's very easy to have doubts.

– In Three Brothers, *the city of Naples is both a real place and a dream place, with the sequence of the young people getting rid of their syringes.*

– The three brothers have different professions: one is a judge, the other a laborer, the third a youth worker in an institution for young offenders in Naples. The youth worker is a man who mainly deals with problems from a moral perspective, not from a technical point of view: how to solve the drug problem. So it's easy to imagine that this man could give way to a visionary attitude. His hopes lead him more to a "vision" than a dream. And so he has this naive

A dramatic image in *Salvatore Giuliano:* **the** *picciotti* **arrested, handcuffed, are led to prison by soldiers of the special corps sent to Sicily.**

A fascinating character – Enrico Mattei – for a moving performance: Gian Maria Volonté in Francesco Rosi's *Il caso Mattei/The Mattei Affair* (on the left, in the role of a journalist, the theater director Luigi Squarzina).

vision of a city that young people clean up, ridding it of all the dangers threatening it; he imagines a more civilized existence for them, full of hope. These young people, living with him in the institution, become at one point the leaders of a great clean-up of the city: all the dangers that threaten it are swept away.

– *The film also used the theme of three cities, Turin for the laborer, Rome for the judge, Naples for the youth worker.*

– At that time Naples was the city experiencing the drug problem most tragically. After that, other cities did too; now the drug problem in Italy is no longer a threat but a reality experienced everywhere and at all social levels. In cities such as Naples and Palermo, drug trafficking is organized crime's principal business.

– *In* Illustrious Corpses, *you use Naples without actually naming the city. Do you feel this city can express the notion itself of what a city is?*

– Yes I think so, since Naples in the eighteenth century was one of the most important capitals of

Europe, and the city has preserved the structure of the great city. When you show Naples, it is the image of a metropolis, not only in terms of the organization of the city, of its urbanism, but also its cultural stratification, a stratification we can see in the façades of its palaces, in the way its streets are planned. I think that the image of Naples is immediately the image of a big city, with all the evils of a big city too.

– *When you're filming, do you feel more comfortable in the city or in the country? Do you feel there are two different ways of looking at reality?*

– When I'm working I feel at ease anywhere where there's a direct rapport between what I want to say and the place that has stimulated me to such a point that I've wanted to make a film there. I never decide to make a film about the countryside or about the city just because the countryside or the city might help me express certain views, or because I like it there myself. In *Three Brothers,* the countryside became an absolutely indispensable element of what I was saying: I wanted to show the problem of the diaspora which began in the fifties

Dialogue between the confined writer (Gian Maria Volonté) and his jailer, the Fascist podestà (Paolo Bonacelli), in Francesco Rosi's *Cristo si è fermato a Eboli/Christ Stopped at Eboli*.

– that internal emigration that cut Italy into two parts even more than, for historical and social reasons, it already was – evoking the abandonment of the countryside was inevitable, with its resulting consequences. In the fifties, the South was emptied of almost five million men, people who represented a considerable work force. The same authorities who during those years supported this emigration and considered it necessary, have today re-evaluated their position: they recognize that this was a very big mistake which caused dramatic consequences of cultural uprooting and the uncontrolled growth of certain cities. Turin, for example, has become the biggest southern city in northern Italy. Internal emigration caused the abandonment of the countryside: young people were attracted by the myth of employment in industries of the North. The Italian rural areas and agriculture were thus impoverished, whereas instead, it would have been possible to develop an industrial plan for the rural South, something that in fact did happen in certain areas, with very positive results. There are particularly flourishing agro-industrial activities in Puglia and even in some parts of Lucania.

Indisputably, a film that manages to expose this problem can be a valuable asset to what is being said about this country's development. And that's why I felt the need to bring the relationship between country and city to the screen in *Three Brothers*. My intention obviously wasn't to show the countryside like a garden of Eden, as a place of delights. The farmer's work has always been, even if today it's a little less so, a very hard job. And in *Christ Stopped at Eboli*, the structure of the story again called for the countryside: with the film's northern intellectual exiled in a small village lost in the most historically distant region of all of Italy, Lucania; who discovers a world perhaps he had never even known existed.

There is no difference, therefore, between shooting in an urban setting or a rural setting. The only problem is to be one with the story you have to tell. I don't know if I've explained what I mean very well. For example, when I went to Spain to make a film about bulls and bullfighters, my knowledge of bullfighting was purely literary. But there again, it was a question of countryside and city. As also in *The Moment of Truth*, there really was the contrast between an industrial city, Barcelona, where it was difficult to find work, and the countryside young men were leaving in the search for fortune. To find true integration, they went back to their roots, that is, to the country. Here, I was saying the same kind of thing as in my other films. Not everything depends upon inspiration, but upon the story you want to tell, not only for yourself, but also in terms of the concerns of the moment. Afterwards, if you take the country, the sea or the city, it's the same.

(SECOND INTERVIEW)

– *Being a film based on a novel particularly famous in Italy* [Christ Stopped at Eboli], *it's difficult not to begin our interview with the problem of adaptation: in his book, Carlo Levi looks back ten years later at a world he had discovered. In the film, however, the description of the character and the experience lived by Levi happen at the same time: it then becomes very difficult to describe and at the same time comment.*

– From a cinematographic point of view, indeed, this posed a great problem. Quite honestly, why had this book never been brought to the screen? From Visconti to De Sica, from Rossellini to Germi, it had been considered a project by many film directors. Nothing ever materialized because every time it was a question of adapting *Christ Stopped at Eboli*, they came up against almost insurmountable difficulties. Neither the public nor cinematographic structures

Always tense and impassioned, Francesco Rosi directs a scene in *Cristo si è fermato à Eboli/Christ Stopped at Eboli* (in the center, Accursio Di Leo).

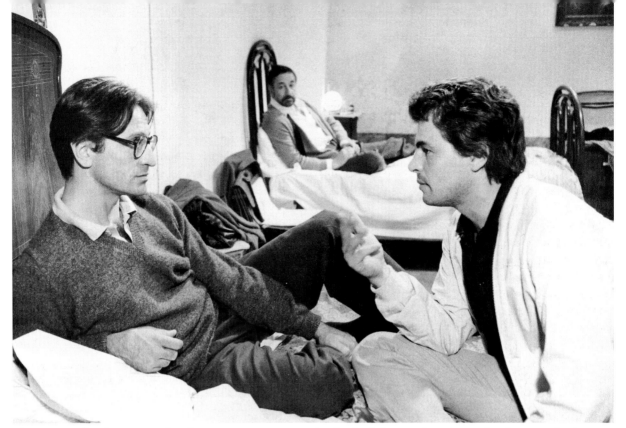

Three émigré brothers reunited in their native Murge upon the death of their mother: the teacher from Naples (Vittorio Mezzogiorno), the judge from Rome (Philippe Noiret), the worker from Turin (Michele Placido), in Francesco Rosi's *Tre fratelli/Three Brothers.*

were ready yet for certain kinds of subjects. Today this has become, I wouldn't say simpler, but more feasible. *Christ Stopped at Eboli* isn't an easy film, but nevertheless, it is certainly a film that manages to establish direct contact with the audience, is emotional, and this, despite the difficulty it represents. There's the entire first part in which I demand the public's undivided attention, I ask them to study the details, the nuances, the looks, the irony that the hero at times expresses, his amazement, his ingenuousness, his innocence... In short, it isn't easy in cinema to make a character expressive who is thinking to himself.

– Another difficulty in the adaptation was that Levi wasn't worried about dramatic progression. For example, at the beginning of his book he relates the episode of a dying peasant which, in the film, you move towards the end.

– That was inevitable: the language of a film is different from the language of a book. For a film, it would have been strange to begin with such a strong episode, an episode that immediately pre-

sents the problem of Levi's medical vocation. The hero is a doctor who, in the beginning, for various reasons refuses his role, and who only little by little begins caring for the sick. The film was to develop this theme, but it was better to do it progressively. The contrary would have been, in my opinion – and also in the screenwriters' opinion who worked with me – a mistake. So, that was one example of the changes that we made to the book's structure; of course we never touched the episodes themselves, nor the spirit of the book.

– In this respect, it seems to me that Levi's sister's visit represents a more obvious rupture in the film than in the book: it is more marked when the hero passes from a contemplative attitude to the attitude of a responsible man.

– This rupture also exists in the book: when Luisa Levi urges her brother to act, the dialogue is directly taken from the author's text in the book. Naturally, the character's contemplative attitude – though at the same time he's thinking to himself – is much more obvious in the film than in the book. While writing,

Levi could continuously mix the description of the village and its inhabitants with his meditation on the problems confronting him. On the contrary, however, in the film the character arrives in the village and sets off on foot to get to know the place where he's going to spend three years of his life in exile: his contemplation is shown in a primary way. This was where the difficulty of making the film arose: to be able to express through images the process of reflection and meditation of a character whose contemplation is apparently the only thing he does. In the first part of the film, the hero devotes himself to a continuous wandering, he sets out walking to get to know the country and the people. You can really say that nothing happens, that there is no action. Apparently nothing happens in the first part of *Eboli*; but in fact, everything happens. Everything happens that will allow the character to express the conclusions of his reflection later on, when he gets the chance to talk to someone of the same cultural and intellectual milieu as he, perhaps like his sister; or to confront a person from a different cultural and intellectual milieu, with whom nevertheless he can establish a relationship, such as the podestà. There are two occasions when the hero can get the spectator to understand what the fruit of his meditation is: he didn't go walking only to contemplate, but also to reflect.

– Before writing the screenplay, did you go to Lucania to see the places where Carlo Levi's story had taken place?

– In my work, I always proceed in a parallel way. I first draw the broad outlines of a structure and then go right away to check right on the site if this structure holds true. After which, I continue the writing with my collaborators. I continue this coming and going right up to the moment I start shooting, between Rome and the place where I'll be filming. These checks in the field are a continual plunge into the materi-al world which I need in order to create a story that's alive and open to the things reality offers. I started doing this with my very first film, *The Challenge*. Having written the screenplay sitting at my desk, when I went to shoot I got such a shock, such a trauma, that I had to start all over again from zero. *Salvatore Giuliano* was the most notable example of this way of working: for this film I used to spend one week in Rome and one week in Sicily. It really wasn't possible to do it any other way. With every trip – I would stay for a week in Montelepre – I would bring back the fruits of my latest hunt: new stories, experiences, testimonies. These trips were even more necessary in a world like the South where the people's mistrust couldn't be overcome all at once. For *Salvatore Giuliano,* this was even truer since the events I wanted to evoke had only occurred about ten years before and were still burning issues: Giuliano's

Just as enthusiastic, in the making of *Carmen:* Francesco Rosi directs Placido Domingo and Julia Migenes-Johnson in Carmen's difficult death scene, murdered by Don José.

sister, brother, mother, Pisciotta's brother, all still lived in Montelepre; all the people in fact, who had been involved in the story that I wanted to tell. Just about everyone regarded me with suspicion. Since I wanted to film in all the real places – I managed to – I had to overcome this suspicion. So, if I hadn't made my stays in Montelepre extend over several months, the consequences would have been very serious: the people would never have become used to me.

– *That kind of familiarity is also precious during the shooting: the inhabitants most likely accept to appear in the film.*

– But of course; all the inhabitants are available since they start considering me as one of them. Little by little, they understand that I want to do an honest job – at least I take the risk of working right in front of them. From that moment on, I understood that for the kind of films I make, continuous confrontation with reality is absolutely indispensable. For *Christ Stopped at Eboli,* having the book at my disposal and knowing the situation at the time, perhaps checks were not as necessary. However, I did them anyway: in my attempt to give the film the weight of human involvement, it was important to establish a continuous rapport with these people, with this land. Otherwise, there was the risk of not understanding them, of not understanding the reasons behind certain things.

– *For* Eboli, *you were only able to shoot one part of the film in Aliano. Did you suffer from the fact that you had to work in several different villages?*

Christ Stopped at Eboli had to be shot in three different villages in order to reconstruct Aliano as described by Levi.

– No, and then, anyway, I didn't have a choice. Aliano was a very small village. The main square of Aliano was inexistent – a few square meters. The changes that had been made since the thirties in this tiny area had truly altered a certain physical reality: electricity transformers, telephone poles, cement walls, new houses, had changed the village a lot. In Aliano, I shot inside the house where Levi had lived, the house with the terraces. The filming was quite complicated; nevertheless, since I worked in three villages that each one had its own distinct situation, this was possible. For example, Levi in his book speaks about an area in complete collapse: today in Aliano, this destroyed area no longer exists. In the film I had to show it, I couldn't be satisfied only alluding to it, as was possible in a book. By chance, I found a village, Craco, where the effects of a landslide could be seen. Craco was larger than Aliano – notably the total site of the collapsed area at the foot of the church was vast – but the small streets, the houses were identical to those in Aliano. The main square in the film was from a third village, Guardia Perticara, that wasn't in the province of Matera, but in the province of Potenza, two hours from there. These three villages offered similar landscapes. This being said, the main landscapes were filmed in Aliano; the clayey land, the deep rocky inlets and ravines, were filmed between Aliano and Alianello.

– *In a certain way, you had to reconstruct the place described by Levi.*

– Frankly, I really think that a film should be examined alone, even when it is based on a book. It's almost necessary to avoid reading the book. Reading is a philological exercise essential from a cultural point of view. However, in terms of the autonomous judgement of a work, books and films are two completely different things.

– *Compared to your previous films, there was a very clear connection between* Christ Stopped at Eboli *and* Uomini contro: *the peasants on the screen were those whom we had seen fighting and suffering in* Uomini contro.

– Yes. Quite honestly, I made *Eboli* in order to pursue further a question with myself. I found elements in Levi's book that I had evoked in my previous films and I thought that the time had come, in the life of my country, to take stock of the situation in the South. There have been so many promises and empty words concerning the South, though the roads that would concretely allow us to resolve the problems haven't been found yet. I would have made a mockery of myself and of those who had cried out with me, if I had expressed myself with the same aggressiveness as my previous films. Today, we can't continue as we did in the past. No, the time has come to incessantly demand, without the slightest equivocation, that the mechanisms are identified which will enable us to resolve the problems of the South. It's not a matter of reflecting just to reflect, but to reflect to find concrete solutions. As denunciation, I think *Eboli* is as forceful as any of my previous films; only the language is different, less direct, but every story needs its own special language.

– *It is quite clear that the film's aim is not to evoke the thirties for their own sake, but to deal with them as a necessary foothold to grasping the complexity of the situation as it exists today.*

– It was to clearly show that despite a certain evolution in the South – an obvious evolution for today's spectator – the fundamental problems have remained identical to those that existed in 1935. The problems of emigration, work, unemployment, agriculture, industrialization, the problem of the region's productive transformation, all of these problems have remained unsolved. Definitely, a certain number of things have changed: the educational situation, sanitation, communications, a certain widespread resemblance between the South and the Nord in terms of mores – nowadays young people are alike in all parts of the world, if not only within Italy. The most important change in the South is that the masses have become aware, they have obtained a civic and political consciousness. This is an important victory that I consider irreversible. But despite this, the South continues to be marginalized; even worse, I'm really afraid that the more the North progresses technologically and in its capacity to exploit labor, the more the South will become distant and excluded. The

The climatic scene from *Cronaca di una morte annunciata* from the famous novel of Gabriel Garcia Marquez. The leading man is Anthony Delon.

South doesn't have the structures to keep up with the North's evolution.

Let's take the example of the educational situation. In Italy, the situation in institutions of learning has evolved greatly over the past thirty years. The university has produced a tremendous number of graduates and post graduates who can't work because the market has nothing to offer. A large number of lawyers, engineers, doctors, can't practice their professions: these people are perhaps the children of those shepherds whom we saw in 1935 and who were still illiterate. Without jobs, unable to remain in the North, these young people return to their villages in the South. There, they're not going to farm since they consider agricultural work below them, that it doesn't have the dignity of the new social level they have acquired thanks to their studies. There is a contradiction here... Courage is needed to clearly confront a certain kind of evolution, for example, the question of *numerus clausus* in the universities. The right to study should be for all – there is absolutely no doubt about it – but this right should be given to those who not only want to continue their studies, but who also have the ca-

pacity. Otherwise, we find ourselves in an absurd, crazy situation, in which students go to take exams by placing a gun on the table in front of the professor. These views tie up with those on Italy's history over the past thirty years: *Eboli* should help us confront this type of questioning. From what the film proposes, it should be possible to start up a discussion, to open a debate.

– Have you participated in public debates in the South?

– Yes, for example in Matera we organized a debate that lasted five hours, with the participation of politicians, intellectuals. A farmer spoke; he was so overcome by the anger of not being able to realize certain things in the right way, nor he or his friends, that at a certain point, he couldn't go on, he wept with rage. His intervention was very dramatic; we filmed it for television.

In these villages in Lucania, Puglia, we find an effort to try to rationalize, to reform, at all levels: the farmers in these regions are very different from those who live close to the big cities such as Naples or Palermo. To find the same rationalization and commitment to trying to solve problems you have to go further away from Naples at least as far as Caserta: the Neapolitan farmer lives very much in the shadow of the urban situation, just as the farmers around Palermo. However in Lucania, in Puglia, in Calabria, the rural factor prevails over the urban factor. Moreover, the farmers' struggles were led for many years by De Vittorio, a man who came from Cerignola, Foggia, Puglia, from a region that has the greatest concentration of agricultural workers and where farmers' struggles after the war were violent: confrontations with the police resulted in deaths among the farmers.

– *Fascism brought no solutions to the problems in the South. As for any changes introduced since 1945, these have modified certain details without bringing any true remedy.*

– Postwar democracy changed certain things in a formal way, others in a substantial way, for example, the construction of a highway system was a substantial transformation; these are important infrastructures. However, the fundamental change is the following: in the past, regions in the South corresponded to depressed areas, truly underdeveloped zones, typical of the Third World. Today, these depressed areas, as a result of a certain type of development that has been applied in Italy, have become assisted areas. The State intervened to assist, but not to offer the employment possibilities that would have solved the problem of productivity in an autonomous way.

– *In the long run, isn't the situation worse than before?*

– Definitely it's worse. This situation eliminates in man a sense of personal responsibility; secondly, this welfare becomes a weight on the shoulders of those who effectively work to support the country; thirdly, this situation creates corporative castes that instead of bringing about the unification of the workers, leads to divisions. We end up with a form of political patronage. Though Italy, because of its contradictions, may be one of the most interesting countries in the world, nevertheless, all of these factors are a very se-

rious threat that weighs upon an effective and profound democratic transformation of the country.

– *In his book, Levi describes a landscape that he is preparing to reproduce on canvas: "Seen from there, the landscape was the least picturesque that I had ever seen, which was why I liked it enormously." In the film, too, you avoid the trap of the picturesque.*

– Certainly. In the same way, I tried to avoid all form of popularity-seeking devices, rhetoric, pitifulness. You might have noticed that I let myself be less impressed than Levi by anything concerning magic, superstitions; I wanted to give more relief to other problems. While trying to avoid the picturesque, I also wanted to show Lucania the way it really was, that is, not only the clayey land, the dust and aridity, but also its bright, splendid nature, as green as the valleys of Ireland or Switzerland, and the marvelous forests that have survived and which at one time completely covered the region. In Lucania, the forest was cut down and was never replanted; the sides of the mountains have thus become very fragile. I conceived things in this way because I felt it was more honest, to this land and to spectators, to show things the way they really were. If I had shown only arid, dry, poor, pale landscapes, I would have exposed the spectator to a kind of blackmail. Instead, I wanted him to be given the means to think for himself and to say: "Here we are in a land covered with grass, trees, goats. How is it possible that we're unable to transform the riches of these natural resources?" By proceeding in this way, I provided the accusers with one more element. A film such as *Eboli* should encourage the spectator to reason on his own. More and more frequently, there has to be a very specific cultural intent backing this kind of film, and this is all the more true the more difficult it becomes to make this type of film: for economic reasons, production is directed towards consumption – something that's happening all over the world. In order to make *Eboli,* I had to make very specific choices and also very specific renunciations: I had to combine all the possibilities I had: TV on the one hand, and Vides de Cristaldi, Action Films, and Gaumont, on the other. I was the one who put together these various contributions, without even being the producer of the film. In short, this film wasn't easy to set up; if I hadn't done things in this way, it is likely that *Eboli* would never have been made at all.

– *There are two versions of* Eboli, *one for cinema that lasts two and a half hours, and one for television that lasts three and a half hours. Are the sequences for television longer, or are there a greater number of sequences?*

– In a way, both. There are more sequences which were planned as such during the writing of the screenplay. For cinema, the film starts with the arrival in exile of the character and ends with his departure. This version follows Levi's story in *Christ Stopped at Eboli.* However, for television, we added a subsequent dialogue between Levi and his sister when the hero is back in Torino, and a dialogue, again in Torino, between Levi and his political friends. With his sister, as well as with his friends, Levi is thus given the opportunity of expressing what the weight of his experience in the South meant, to speak of this experience and to theorize. In the film, these sequences would have seemed like a repetition: in fact, if people hadn't understood the meaning of the film, a later reflection was useless. However, for television, *Eboli* was to be broadcast in four episodes, one each week. Perhaps many people wouldn't see them all, so, in the last episode, there was the kind of theorizing, notably ideological, that resumed somewhat what Levi had lived and what had been shown in the film.

So that's why there's a slight difference between the conception of the film, and the program presented on television. The two sequences with the sister and the friends lasted twenty to twenty-five minutes. The other half hour consisted of some scenes that weren't included in the film, for example, a sequence of "saltarello" that was part of peasant life, or a farewell scene between the priest and Levi. Levi meets Don Trajella while coming back from the house of the dying peasant, he passes in front of the little church where the priest has been sent and there is a rather touching sequence: these two men want to say a lot of things to each other, but they say absolutely nothing; it's an almost completely silent scene. There was also a sequence where Levi is painting and does a portrait of Giulia: Giulia teaches him a poem and, during the night, he recites this poem again. Then, here and there, there were little cuts that I thought were necessary to give the cinematographic version an acceptable length.

– Y*ou hadn't worked again with Raffaele La Capria since* Uomini contro. *What made you choose him again?*

– Usually I work with Tonino Guerra, who is my official collaborator. Then, depending on the different films I undertake, I call upon other screenwriters. For *Eboli* it seemed to me that La Capria – with whom I have made several films – was particularly suited to collaborate with me, that he could become involved in a film like this.

Sergio Leone

– Once Upon a Time in America *exudes total control, most likely due to the subtle way the film is constructed.*

– I think *Once Upon a Time in America* was a movie that on paper should really have scared any producer away, the film was so anticonformist. It was above all the very meager, very short story of the life of a minor figure in the history of organized crime. When I read the novel, *The Hoods*, by Harry Grey, with the part about his youth (since, of course, the novel didn't continue up to today, it ended with the death of the three friends caused by the error of the fourth), I immediately wanted to make a movie out of it. In actual fact, things hadn't really happened as in the book. I met Harry Grey, and it was quite an exploit since at first his lawyer was against my meeting him. But then, it so happened that Grey was one of my fans, he had seen my films; and so he said to me, "I'll come, but I'll be alone and you must be alone, too." I told him that I couldn't because my English wasn't good enough and I needed to bring an interpreter. So I went with my brother-in-law and it was good that I met him: that was what made me decide to make the movie. Grey told me that he had written his anti-Hollywood book while he was a prisoner at Sing Sing. Nevertheless, to me the book sounded more like the voice-over of some bad Hollywood screenwriter. Grey had remained so fascinated by Hollywood cinema that unconsciously all the quotes, allusions, adventures and even psychological overtones came from movies he had seen. The most fascinating part of the book, the truest, most authentic, is definitely the part about his childhood, the one that is most anecdotal. Afterwards, he doesn't reveal all the truth about his grown-up years: a lot of things stayed in the closet.

– *When was* The Hoods *published?*

– The book was published in the fifties, in 1955, I think. It was reasonably successful, but nothing great. They must have sold about two million copies in paperback in the United States. Grey continued to write more books, for example, *Call Me Duck*, a work in which he just rehashed the same things; whatever he wasn't able to fit into the first book was included in the second.

– *Had anyone thought of making a screenplay out of Harry Grey's book?*

– Embassy Pictures had thought of it, and that was my dilemma, my problem. John Levine had bought the rights. Then he resold them to an American director, Dan Curtis, the one who later made the series, *The Winds of War*. Curtis never wanted to sell the rights. Initially I had started talking about the film with Génovès here in Paris. We contacted Curtis and he said no. And then the project was handed over to Grimaldi who turned out to be extremely astute: Grimaldi told him that he would finance another film if Curtis sold the rights. And so it was done. Afterwards, with Grimaldi, there was a whole series of complications that held me up for three or four years. Grimaldi was in a bad way because of Fellini's *Casanova* and Bertolucci's *1900*, two films that had led to a suit with the Americans. For me, things started looking up when Arnon Milchan got involved, the Israelian who eventually produced *Once Upon a Time in America*.

– *With the passing of the years had the final screenplay become very different from the first adaptation?*

– Yes, it had changed a lot. For example, there were, shall we say, historical things in the 1968 part that were clearly understandable; with the passing of the years, they became less so. We eliminated those. Initially the film was supposed to begin in a completely different way. I had written the first part with an American screenwriter who afterwards made a movie with Frankenheimer; he practically stole that whole first part by giving it to John

Frankenheimer's *99 and 44/100 Dead*. The film was released and it was a bad film; there's this sequence in the beginning that I wanted to do, a cemetery along the Hudson River. So, we changed the original screenplay a lot. I first started writing with Medioli and Arcalli, and then Arcalli died and I worked with Benvenuti and De Bernardi. I gave them all the childhood part, a little because I remembered a film that they had written with Franco Rossi, *Friends for Life*. Ferrini did the last part, that is, he collaborated with us on the writing of the final script, but the treatment was already finished when he joined.

– Did the long period of waiting and the screenplay's long development help the film?

– I don't know. One thing is absolutely sure: the way it was conceived, the film was more than *one* film, really it was two. Grimaldi, in fact, was hoping it would become two long episodes, a bit like *1900*, and this, for better or for worse, was something that remained. Even after the cuts, it was constructed like that. This was so true that I still have an hour more to add for TV, an hour already edited but not dubbed, that would make the film four and a half hours long. Maybe you can tell where it was cut... Nevertheless, the film is rigorously structured. Clearly, the film might be a little bitter to taste, since it is born out of nothingness, that is, out of the limbo of opium. There's this character who appears and who, suddenly, in twenty minutes of the film, goes into oblivion and returns without the public knowing the characters' or story's background. Then little by little there's a long flashback to his childhood, which to me is crucial, since

Charlie Chaplin with Franco Zeffirelli and Sergio Leone: a link between Europe and America.

childhood, of course, is the platform for the entire story of this great friendship between two characters. It's a little like *Once Upon a Time in the West*, a dance of death with a man plunging into oblivion. If the film had a subtitle, it could also be called, "Once Upon a Time a Certain Kind of Cinema." It's a homage to things that have interested me; we find here a preoccupation with death which, after fifty, comes automatically. I see that I've started reading the obituary columns now, though I never read them before.

– Noodles, the hero, is a rather ordinary person.

– This is really what I liked about the character and the author of the book, this poor man who, at the end of his life, at seventy years of age, was still forced to hide out. Perhaps, in fact, it was his wife, a schoolteacher, who wrote the book and he just dictated his memoirs to her. No one would ever have written about him if he hadn't decided to write something himself. This is the America which I find the most fascinating, that intrigues me the most, that interests me the most, these minor figures... Someone like Grey seems as if he were seen through the window of a café; America flows over his body without ever being able to touch or change him.

– By having Robert De Niro play the part, wasn't there the risk of seeing the actor give more substance to the character, making him into something more than just a minor figure in the history of American organized crime?

– Clearly, the film was entirely in the hands of a great actor's interpretation. So I ran the risk of having the character turn out differently. This being said, De Niro is also like a chameleon, the only actor capable of playing Mr. Nobody convincingly. My first choice had been De Niro. I had thought of him fourteen years ago when he wasn't a big star yet, just after having seen him in Scorsese's *Mean Streets*. Maybe that was what made him accept the part, the fact that he had been chosen – the first time that I phoned him – when the proposal wasn't suspicious. It is true that I allowed myself things with De Niro that wouldn't have been as easy with

another actor. It's as if all the dialogues in the world and all the anxieties in the world are painted on that face.

– Robert De Niro has a face that is at the same time anonymous and incredibly unique.

– Indeed, that was what we were betting on. That's also why the film has its own, shall we say, special length; the close-ups had to be insistent, longer than normal, to truly give the sensation that I had in mind.

– Did the shooting go smoothly?

– We worked in perfect symbiosis; everything went marvelously. I have my rhythms, he has his and at certain times they coincide: so, there weren't any problems.

– Choosing James Woods to play alongside Robert De Niro must have presented quite a few difficulties.

– James Woods was as good as his role was difficult. In the beginning we had thought of Dustin Hoffman to play Max. I even spent three days with Hoffman, from morning to night, but he, in fact, really wanted the part of Noodles. It was difficult to have an actor playing opposite De Niro – especially a De Niro so committed and so mature – who couldn't pull his own weight. Our choice therefore was risky. I had seen James Woods in *The Onion Field* and had already noticed him a few years before in *Holocaust*. I had him do a test and saw this face... I liked Woods because he had a face that reminded one of a slightly hard and mean Leslie Howard. This romantic side with, however, this hoodlum side that he had in the look in his eyes and in the shape of his mouth, made him correspond perfectly to the features of Max's personality.

– How long did the shooting take?

– It lasted six or seven months, with a few short breaks and one month devoted to traveling. In fact, *Once Upon a Time in America* is equal to two films. If you consider that I shot *Once Upon a Time in the West* in fourteen weeks, automatically I needed thirty for this one. The movie was shot in New York in the Lower East Side, that is, below the bridge shown in the film, the Williamsburg that virtually binds Brooklyn to the Lower East Side, all the Jewish quarter too, described in the book.

– Did you encounter any particular problems while working in New York?

– No problems. At first I was really afraid because everyone had told me that, the neighborhood now being occupied by the Puerto Ricans, I was going to run into problems. But, in fact, the Puerto Ricans were especially helpful; perhaps the fact that we were Italians and belonged to a minority too, helped. I went to see them before shooting, I spoke to them and discovered that basically the fears were more what Americans felt out of racism than based on true

fact. In reality, these poor people stayed for four months with their windows covered up by our store-front sets and said nothing in exchange for a miserable sum of money. They were really good people and I must say that in this respect everything went very well. However, I did have problems with the motion picture unions, difficulties you find every-where, including on a political level. We had accepted to work with a minority union. All the American crew that appears in the credits, in fact, I never used. I let them all stay at home after paying their wages. By using a minority union, I could hire slightly fewer people. The majority union got mad and made themselves heard through some influential voices, Reagan's and Ted Kennedy's, who had been called to the rescue. The union ran an out- and-out campaign with declarations such as, "When America has economic problems how can an Italian crew be al-

Gangsters and unions. Treat Williams, Robert De Niro, Richard Bright, William Forsythe in *Once Upon a Time in America*.

lowed to invade the country?" In fact, we left before the scheduled date...

– You also shot part of the film in Canada.

– There, I worked under very good conditions since, as it turned out, I was a good friend of Trudeau and also Drapeau, the mayor of Montreal. I was able to work in Montreal as if I had been in Rome. They were very helpful people. In Canada I shot a number of sequences, the boat cemetery where the shoot-out takes place, the car scene at the beginning with the fire and the three people burned to death, the hospital scene, outside the federal bank with the cars passing by, the newsstand fire. I shot all of them in real places with things brought over, windows, cornices; a tremendous amount of work carried out with Carlo Simi and the Italian crew, very good collaborators, who all came over from Italy. Moreover, I did the same thing in the States when I shot *Once Upon a Time in the West* or when I produced *My Name is Nobody*. For the latter we went to a small long-lost town, the same one where *Easy Rider* was shot – it was Peter Fonda who told me this – and rebuilt an Indian village with earth and mud exactly like the natives did. The Italian builders copied the Indians using their primitive techniques in the work.

– The rest of the film was made in Italy.

– No, I also filmed in Paris. I did the New York Central Station sequence there, which was an imitation of the Gare du Nord in Paris, with the same large glass roofs. Since the station didn't exist anymore in New York, I shot it at the Gare du Nord. I also filmed a scene which I cut from the release version but which is included in the four-and-a-half-hour one. It was a scene that takes place in the beautiful restaurant in the station and which, in fact, I shot at Chez Julien, the famous Rue Saint-Denis bistrot. From a photographic point of view, this scene is marvelous. In Italy, I shot in Venice. I filmed the inside and the outside of the Hotel Excelsior and the beach. Long Island was like that, with lots of thirties Moorish-style buildings that stretched all the way to Atlantic City. Having at hand, on the Lido of Venice, perhaps the most most

superb specimen, it was only natural that I use it. And then I filmed in Como, in an American's house: the interior resembled those of the Long Island houses very much and it's the one you see at the end of the movie, the reception given in Max's residence. As for the rest, I built all the interiors at Cinecittà, the opium den, Fat Moe's bar, the speakeasy, etc. We even had to build Fat Moe's place twice, the first one on a lot at Cinecittà, a true-scale construction with the outside and the adjacent alley and also all the interiors; and then the second one, which you see from the outside on the rare occasions that we're in the real streets of New York. So, we built two twin sets, one that we sent to America, and the other that we used in Italy.

– How do you work with your designer Carlo Simi? What kinds of instructions do you give him?

– Extreme care is taken so that the sets are built true-to-life, a piece taken from here, another from a different place. I use photos of the period a lot. I do meticulous research that amazes even my closest American friends like Scorsese or Spielberg. When they came to Rome they were surprised at all these photographs, by this exhaustive documentation that started off from specific detail to finally obtain a total effect. Look at Fat Moe's bar, what care, this central kitchen rebuilt at Cinecittà, with all the objects brought over from New York, the scales... Absolutely everything was recreated meticulously. With Carlo, we have long discussions, we talk over everything, then he custom builds. For example, you've seen the photographic studio where the boys get together with the large glass window and the curtains, well, it's something that is taken from a real decor, a New York studio that I liked and had rebuilt exactly the same. Fat Moe's apartment where, at the beginning of the film, Noodles goes to ask for a room to sleep in, is the same set, but reduced and refurnished. This set went through various metamorphoses. For the sequence on the terrace I was very lucky. In New York's Little Italy I found a 360° panorama intact with all the old buildings in wood and very few television antennas: I removed about twenty, though I could have found five thousand on those roofs. That was really an extraordinary stroke of luck. All of these sets represent incredible work, that would be almost impossible to repeat again.

– *I imagine you are just as demanding when it comes to the costume designer, Gabriella Pescucci.*

– Yes, of course. I took costumes from three different places: New York, Los Angeles and England. Uniforms from some places, civilian clothes from others, all authentic costumes. I also asked Tirelli who, in Rome, had 1920-25 costumes and then all of Visconti's costumes... I really work in perfect harmony with my collaborators on the sets, costumes, props. Nothing is left to chance. For example, if there's a character with a brown jacket on the set, I might ban certain colors, reds, blues. I screen everything. When Noodles drinks a coffee, he doesn't use a round cup but a hexagonal cup with little flowery thirties designs.

– *The sets and costumes are highlighted by director of photography Tonino Delli Colli's work.*

– Delli Colli is very good; he created fabulous photography for *Once Upon a Time in America,* he managed to capture the atmosphere of three different periods. Thanks to RN, Delli Colli could play with the different eras, the twenties with the children; 1933 with pastel colors; finally our own times with sequences set in 1968. RN is a well-known Technicolor process that's a little more expensive but can help you obtain much deeper blacks and much more luminous whites. This process was an Italian Technicolor invention. That was why Warren Beatty's *Reds* was printed in Italy, two or three thousand copies whose printing was done in Rome instead of Hollywood.

– *Did you shoot with live sound?*

– Generally, we shot with live sound. Though I'm a little responsible for the damages suffered as a result of direct recording. I work with music, I try things out by playing music on the set. Before the shooting begins, I ask Ennio Morricone to compose original themes, something I've done since *The Good, the Bad and the Ugly.* Someone told me

that Kubrick tried exactly the same thing with *Barry Lyndon.* Naturally, when I'm filming, we cut the music. Sometimes, when the actor is taken by the music, he'll ask me to keep the music going during the shooting because he gets more sensations from the music. In fact, music is a big help to actors, especially in the love scenes. So, at times I've shot with the music, when De Niro or other actors have asked me to. We knew that later we would have to dub the scene. Most of the film was recorded with live sound by a Frenchman, Jean-Pierre Ruh, the sound man for *Tess.*

– *How much of the final editing of* Once Upon a Time in America *is live sound?*

– The scenes recorded live are between 60 to 70 percent of the film. We dubbed about 35 percent of the whole film. This wasn't a very big problem since all the actors were very good, Robert De Niro to begin with. So, when he asked to keep the music it was because he was sure he would be just as good dubbing. For now, we haven't done the dubbing yet of the extra hour of the long version, but with American actors it's easy: you call them up and they come. It's the actors close by, the French, the Italians, who are harder to get a hold of!

– *In the credits we see "Additional dialogues by Stuart Kaminsky." What was Kaminsky's role?*

– Kaminsky is a film historian; he lives in Chicago and has also written detective novels on cinema. He was one of my fans and I knew his books. For the film, I needed someone Jewish, Polish or of Polish ancestry who knew a little Yiddish and also how to write. Kaminsky was perfect. What was our problem? The film had been structured and written in Italian; we went through a translator who, no matter how good – which was our case – limits himself to the work of a translator. The screenplay then had to be given to a writer. I chose Kaminsky for these reasons: first of all, he knew me well; secondly, he wrote detective stories; thirdly, he knew motion pictures. So, I asked him to revise the dialogues. His participation was limited, of a technical nature. He didn't add anything; he faithfully and freely adapted certain parts that seemed too "translated."

– Apart from your period of pseudo-historic epics, you have worked exclusively with themes based on America. Can you explain this preference?

– A bit by chance. In the days when I was working as an assistant, the big productions were made by the Americans. I was a rather unique assistant director because I didn't speak English. In order to work I needed a translator, so the producer paid me and also the interpreter. I worked with a lot of Americans – Wise, Wyler, Zinnemann, Walsh, Mervyn Le Roy. I rubbed shoulders with more or less all of them during the Roman Hollywood period.

– After the fall of Fascism and right after the war, Italian intellectuals were extremely interested in America. How did you live this phenomenon?

– I lived it in a strange way since by background I was a neorealist. I started out with De Sica; my first film was *The Bicycle Thief.* Then, I worked with other directors, Camerini, Comencini, Soldati, Bonnard and even the veteran Gallone. When the Americans arrived on the scene I discovered a type of cinema that interested me. Let's be honest: I was impatient to break out of neorealism. For me, cinema is imagination. Movies can successfully express things through the resources of the fable. I have

Sergio Leone during the shooting of *Once Upon a Time in America*.

never liked ideological films because I don't think they really serve much purpose. Cinema should express itself through its own means, and then also smuggle across ideas and desires, under the condition that they are just, and without putting pressure on the public. My encounters, for example with Wise, Walsh or Zinnemann, were fundamental to me, above all in showing me how a certain type of cinema was made. That's the technical side. But I also learned a lot by collaborating on a variety of different kinds of films, the religious tale of *The Nun's Story* to *Ben Hur.* I think this helped me discover a kind of cinema that could carry a message and at the same time be spectacular.

– Among your films as assistant I believe you also worked with Emile Couzinet.

– That's right, I wasn't Couzinet's assistant, I was his advisor for the Italian version – the one who claimed the authorship of the film for Italy. It was in 1954, thirty years ago, for a film called *Quai des illusions* with Fausto Tozzi and Lise Bourdin. The film was shot in Bordeaux where Couzinet had his empire. I remember that it was his first film in CinemaScope and he thought that he had made a mistake: when he saw the rushes, since he didn't know how to use the CinemaScope lenses, he found he had gotten very small characters, long shots, whereas what he had wanted were close-ups. And so he said, "They fooled me." I explained that all you had to do was change the lens and get closer to the actors with the camera...

– In Once Upon a Time in America, *beyond its qualities as entertainment, we discover a particular political vision of America.*

– Indeed, I think the Americans object a little to the film for this as well, and not only because of its length. This is so true that I'm now in a suit with them and I don't know how it's all going to turn out. It seems they want to cut it by an hour and slavishly edit it in chronological order. Nothing will be left of the film then, it'll become "The Godfather N° 18." I think they have a very definite intention there. The film relates a personal story but this story also serves as a pretext so that, as it sediments,

a certain way of seeing America appears. It is obvious that Max represents certain powers that in America resemble him. One day, a young Jewish filmmaker said to me, "Why don't you make a film on the American Constitution, that democratic constitution that leaves so many blanks between one article and another?" In fact in America, appealing to the Fifth Amendment keeps people like Al Capone from ever being charged with what they have really done – mass murder – and, if you want to corner them, you have to get them for tax fraud. This proves that from the start the Constitution was well studied to allow for this type of situation.

– Was depicting the Jewish milieu just by chance? Or only because this was the starting point of Grey's book?

– Yes, it was by chance; only because the book talks about it. It's a milieu of Jewish gangsters. In reality, Harry Grey's name was Goldberg and he was a Jew who, I think, worked in perfect symbiosis with the Italians. In the book he constantly cites a certain Frankie, a character that I included in the film in a short sequence. This Frankie was most probably Frank Costello. So I think Grey must have been one of Costello's men.

– Does specifically Jewish gangsterism exist?

– Yes, it exists, though it is always mixed, like you see in *The Godfather.* You remember the character played by Lee Strasberg: he portrayed that gangster who died four months ago in Miami. In fact, he was the boss of the boss, the one from Cuba. In *The Godfather* he had a fictitious name but he actually did exist.

– Do you think that the minorities in the American population were more responsible for organized crime?

– All I know is one thing: we exported farmers and we imported gangsters. That's really the truth. It can be explained as a certain way the immigrants protested, it can be explained by Sacco and Vanzetti, by the way certain minorities in America are treated, Lice Island, the most dreadful hunger.

These people went over there dreaming of an America and later found themselves confronted with a very different reality and situation. That some abused of this state of affairs doesn't justify becoming criminals, but it was definitely a little because of this. People descend into crime, little by little, they are victimized once, then twice... and then finally they say no. In *The Godfather* this evolution was shown very well. We should also add that, in effect, the people who emigrated were those who would absolutely not tolerate offenses: a Sicilian has a hard time tolerating certain repression, the same goes for an Irishman. And because of this, these were the men who reacted the most violently and who later became criminals. And, moreover, they understood the corruption there perfectly well. They adapted to the world in which they found themselves. That's how I see it, and I think it's the truth. There's also something else extremely fascinating about the Italians. The Jews were much more intelligent; they were always more or less behind the desk, taking advantage of the Italians' taste for putting on a show. The Italian is more theatrical, he likes to go out in the street. But the most important figure in American crime during the past years, someone who was higher up than Lucky Luciano or Al Capone, the one who pulled all the strings of the entire organization, was a Jew.

The Italians had quite a lucid and productive example to follow, the clerical hierarchy. They already knew that you started from the priest, and then you needed the bishop, the cardinal, until you could finally reach, after various filters, right up to the Pope. If then, the Pope gave an order – since in the clergy, orders were not discussed but executed – the cardinal had to do what he had to do, and the bishop the same, and the priest the same. This implied a solid defense. I remember an anecdote that I wanted to put in the film, then finally I didn't, or rather I had Noodles say about his disappearance,

Ready for action: James Woods, Robert De Niro, James Hayden, William Forsythe in *Once Upon a Time in America*.

Robert De Niro (Noodles), young and old, in *Once Upon a Time in America*.

"I went into the world's ass-hole for thirty-five years, for all those years I went to bed much too early." Anyway, there were two partners in Chicago; the Organization called one of the two and ordered him to kill the other. He didn't argue; he went and killed him. It was understood that after the murder he would leave his car and get into one of the Organization's cars that would drive him to a safe place. After the murder, however, the man got out of his car and, instead of getting into the car following him, he dashed into the woods nearby and disappeared. After thirteen years, he was found in Hollywood, working as an extra in a costume epic. This man had left everything, house, loved ones, work, since he knew that just the way he had killed his partner, he would also have been killed. So, you never escape from the Organization, even if you leave, even if you run away, if you lose yourself in the void...

– In the Mafia, kisses on the hand or on the mouth also seem to me to have religious origins.

– Yes, of course, it comes from the Italian nature of the Mafia, it's the Italian side of the organized crime world; the Jewish side is the one of big insurance policies. For example, if you lend a mil-

lion dollars to someone, you take out an insurance for a million and a hundred thousand dollars. If the person disappears or dies, the lender gets back a hundred thousand dollars more. Sometimes it happens that the borrower is killed after his reimbursement; the lender then recovers twice the amount, plus a hundred thousand dollars. These practices exist...

– The stories of both Noodles and Max are parallel, their lives are both failures.

– *Once Upon a Time in America* is indeed a very bitter film; it ends in a life's total failure. The other character remains bound to the only possibility that he has, that of, until thirty, having lived a friendship that he doesn't want to cut himself off from. I'm a European director and can only be fascinated with America by what I've read, studied. Of course, through the film you find all my memories of Chandler, Hammett, Dos Passos, Fitzgerald, etc. So, this adventure of Noodles, this dream, this search through time, and this disillusionment; his advance towards death, can only be, with the final scene – the flashback when Noodles goes into the opium den – a voyage induced by opium. Opium projects you more towards the future than to the past. The film thus makes a dual reading possible – here I say it, and here I deny it – and may represent what the character imagines under the effect of the drug: in 1933, with his act of informing, Noodles is morally and physically dead.

– So the film, far from being realistic, might in fact be completely oneiric?

– Certainly. That this dream be questionable in terms of reality, doesn't really matter to me. For me, reality, too, is a dream. Obviously, the implications in *Once Upon a Time in America* are of a much different nature than the slavish relating of one person's story or chronicle.

– The editing of the film helps to read it on two levels.

– This was done on purpose; so that the spectator would lose any specific reference points that would help him recognize the period he was in. This was done very carefully.

– *To go back to more technical questions, do you work with only one camera or with several?*

– Sometimes I work with two or three cameras. For interiors, Tonino Delli Colli asked me not to use a second camera. It helped him to adjust the light better: when the light is studied for one kind of shot, it won't be as good for the others. Several cameras are better for newsreels. For exteriors, these problems don't exist, so I always use two or three cameras. For the interiors, since the first cameraman wanted it, and out of respect for his work – in this case, of exceptional quality – I generally only used one.

– *Do you sometimes use a video camera to check the framing and the development of a scene?*

– No, because video cameras distract me. I'm already distracted by the Moviola. I hate television, little screens. A video camera is a help so that you don't have to rely on the cameraman's opinion, especially for someone demanding like me. When I ask him how's the angle, he trembles... Nevertheless, I prefer taking the risk, and even redoing a shot the next day if something really isn't right, rather than use a video camera. But with Carlo Tafani, I didn't have any problems: he is incredibly skillful; he's a monster; he managed to do traveling shots for me with no problem at all, taking the Ariflex in hand and getting magnificent shots. So I trusted him totally. I like to be in front of the actor while I'm looking at him; if I'm watching the monitor carefully I lose all the details, all the subtleties of his acting, of his way of performing, everything that he expresses when you look at him. With De Niro it was wonderful because he uses the director, at least I got this sensation, like a mirror. With him, you can't have anyone behind the camera, not even the cameraman. The cameraman has to disappear, to hide. When De Niro is acting, he must not have anyone in view. Nevertheless, the figure, let's call it charismatic, of the director tied to the camera, seemed for him to be a necessity. I often told him, "If I bother you, I can hide too; it's not a problem for me; I'll go behind the camera." But instead, he really wanted the unique presence of this person there, really watching him, as if he were being reflected in a mirror. And this was very beautiful.

– *Have you ever thought of shooting anything for television?*

– I already told you, I hate the little screen, I hate television, I hate the Moviola, I hate anything that limits, that reduces, that constrains, and even, in a way, exorcizes and leads to fanaticism. I didn't see *Terms of Endearment* but I have the feeling that it is a story inspired by telefilms, the result of *Dallas* and the likes. And this film gets five Oscars! And so people see these kinds of movies on TV and then go to see them at the cinema...

– *So you strongly defend cinema's independence from television.*

– People can say anything they like about *Once Upon a Time in America*, they can criticize it, but no one can say that there isn't a love of cinema in this film. As long as I'm allowed to, this is the kind of film I'm going to make. An Italian critic who saw the movie said to me, "It seems as if it were made with a lens of nostalgia; you used a new lens to say that perhaps we wouldn't be seeing this kind of film anymore." On the other hand, I also understand the producers and I understand the massive intervention of television, but I won't justify it at all, moreover: I hate it and I'll struggle against it with all my might, in order to put off its triumph for as long as possible. I imagine bigger and bigger, more gigantic screens in homes for certain types of special films. In fact, in Japan, they already build a fifth partition in the living room which is a full screen. I also imagine a stadium, that is, only five projectors in a big city – the opposite of what they're doing in France, where old theaters are broken up into ten auditoriums – I imagine films screened before ten thousand, twenty thousand people. This would correspond to the need to get together to "eat cinema," "live cinema." Already, successfully, there are events being organized such as the Basilica of Massenzio in Rome. I had the pleasure of seeing, at Massenzio, *Once Upon*

Once Upon a Time in America. The film's adolescents in the streets of New York.

a *Time in the West* shown on a thirty-meter screen with five thousand spectators. I was moved, the person who made the film was moved, imagine the others...

– Do you think you're going to make another film soon?

– I hope to make another film right away. I'm difficult when it comes to choosing because, in fact, I need pretexts more than stories; and it's not easy to find the right pretext. Nevertheless, I hope I find it soon because I don't want to play the producer anymore. I was born to be behind the camera; I think that's the only work for me.

Bernardo Bertolucci

(FIRST INTERVIEW)

– In 1962 you became known for two simultaneous successes; your first film, The Grim Reaper, *and your anthology of poems,* In cerca del mistero, *which was awarded the Viareggio prize for new writers. Was there a point in your life when you hesitated between cinema and literature?*

– When I was a child people sometimes asked me, "What do you want to do when you grow up?" I answered, "I want to make movies." In the meantime, since there was a poet in the house, my father, Attilio Bertolucci, I started composing poetry as soon as I learned how to write, that is, from the age of six. So, this could be seen as a very strong emulation of my father. However, as my father was also a film critic in a provincial town – Parma – I often used to go with him to see movies that he was supposed to review. I even identified Parma with cinema since we lived in the country and only went to Parma, in fact, to see movies. When I was about fourteen I received a 16mm camera and made my first film, a fifteen-minute movie with a narrative. I made another one [1] when I was sixteen. By the time I turned twenty, making movies seemed quite natural. When you think that something is natural, it's also natural that it comes naturally. So, in 1961 – I was twenty – I became Pasolini's assistant for *Accattone.*

– How did you meet Pasolini?

– My father published Pasolini's first novel in 1955, *Ragazzi di vita,* and then the anthology of poems... My father, who worked for the great publisher Garzanti, helped Pasolini out a lot in his early

Bernardo Bertolucci, the filmmaker of intimate sufferings and great historical frescoes.

years. And this was how I became Pasolini's friend who, in fact, lived for many years in the same building as we did, on the ground floor. When I was sixteen, I used to write poems and went running downstairs to show them to Pasolini. He's the one who encouraged me to have them published. So, between us we had a very classic and traditional relationship of mentor and pupil. When Pasolini made his first film, he called me to be his assistant. Pasolini came from literature, from novels, poetry, criticism, semantics; however, I was closer to cinema. Nevertheless neither one of us had done anything in applied cinematography; those two 16mm films I spoke about before were really amateur films. So, I was his assistant for *Accattone* and what was I witness to? I was witness to the invention of cinema: Pasolini had invented a language.

Accattone was very important for me since it was very rare to be able to witness a new language being invented: in Pasolini's case, it was truly an

---

[1] These were two shorts, *Morte di un maiale* and *La teleferica.*

invention, since he had no important cinematographic culture to draw upon; there was none. At the time, the only film he really liked was Dreyer's *The Passion of Joan of Arc*. Afterwards, he started going to the movies more often. So, to repeat something I've said many many times before, the first day Pasolini did a traveling shot, I really had the feeling I was seeing the first traveling in the history of cinema. After that, *Accattone* became a success and Pasolini sold a story to Antonio Cervi. This producer asked me to write a screenplay based on the story and to direct it. It was *The Grim Reaper*.

– During those years what films struck you the most?

– The same ones which I'm still struck by today, Renoir, Dovjenko, Godard, Mizoguchi, Rossellini and a lot of American cinema from the twenties, thirties, forties, fifties. By then I had already been going to the Cinémathèque Française a lot, I was very interested in cinema...

– Accattone, *though being the work of a new director, nevertheless shows great stylistic maturity.*

– Pasolini had decided to be a primitive, a very perverse choice as well as being a very genuine one. He didn't know very much about cinema, or he knew it badly. He used to go to the movies off-handedly... without any serious interest. The great maturity in *Accattone* was due to the fact that Pasolini was not at all worried about avant-garde cinema. He was very free while shooting the film; his references were more pictorial than cinematographic – pictorial and oneiric, Masaccio, Giotto, and their dreams. In *Mamma Roma,* there's Mantegna; in *Accattone*

In 1961, twenty-year-old Bernardo Bertolucci worked as assistant director for neighbor Pier Paolo Pasolini on the mythical set of *Accattone*.

the point of reference – all those close-ups – was really Masaccio.

– *Was the reference to Masaccio conscious?*

– Yes, absolutely. And then, there was the influence of dreams. I remember that every morning on our way to the place where we were shooting, he would tell me about the dreams he had had the night before. In a way, these dreams influenced his work during the day.

– *This style of working highlights cinema's dual nature, as a language of the dream and as an objective language, born out of reality, that goes out to meet the camera.*

– In dreams just as in cinema, or in cinema just as in dreams, we are very free to surrender ourselves to free associations. Cinema is truly a language that uses signs from real life. Pasolini used to say that the language of cinema was life itself. Cinema is made of very crude material woven on a loom of dreams. For this reason I find moviemaking much closer to poetry than to prose, to music than to theater. Even cinema at its seemingly most theatrical uses the theater as a ruse, as a disguise.

Alvaro D'Ercole and Romano Labate in Bertolucci's *La commare secca/The Grim Reaper.*

– *When you wrote the screenplay of* The Grim Reaper, *did you feel completely free with Pasolini's story?*

– Well, I felt that, through my writing, I had to gain possession of a story which in the beginning had belonged to someone else. I therefore tried to absorb Pasolini's story. I wrote the screenplay of *The Grim Reaper* with Sergio Citti, who was Pasolini's collaborator, in order to keep my feet on the ground and never falsify the reality described by Pasolini. Nevertheless, I think that while shooting I was attracted and inspired by different things: I was already beginning to get a confused idea of my own identity as a film director. And so, I was very irritated – I was very young then, I was twenty-one – whenever anyone said that *The Grim Reaper* was a Pasolinian film. It was a film about things of very minor importance compared to the significant themes dealt with in for example, *Accattone*, which is a little like a Greek tragedy. My film is also a film about death – "commare secca" means death

All the energy of a director at work, Bernardo Bertolucci.

in Roman dialect – though here it was perhaps seen in a more lyrical, more crepuscular way than in Pasolini. I lacked Pier Paolo's sense of sacredness, and I still do. In *The Grim Reaper,* the scent of death was rendered more in the way I structured the film, a film entirely based upon the passing of time and its consuming of everything, but this didn't show. The idea was a little like the famous remark by Cocteau: "Cinema is catching death at work." It's strange, but today I was reading *Opium* in which Cocteau says that each of his books guillotine all other preceding books. This vision of guillotined books is beautiful. Close-ups are like the guillotine. So in *The Grim Reaper,* a storm takes each of the characters by surprise in a different place, with a different friendship, in a different situation. I really wanted to show the workings of time: which, in a way, is just how death works, that is, time passes and death labors. The storm gave unity to everything, recalled death, and death, the convention, was washed by the rain: at twenty-one, in fact, I considered myself immortal.

– *How was* The Grim Reaper *received in Italy?*

– The film was quite successful. In addition, it was a film that hadn't cost a lot. *The Grim Reaper* was shown at the Venice Film Festival. A few days before the film was presented there, I had been awarded the Viareggio prize for my book of poetry. I was too young; it seemed impossible to have a book win an award at Viareggio and have a film presented at Venice. In a way it was scandalous. The film was received with certain reservations and this was how I first discovered the conformity of film critics. Moreover, I discovered something else that was scandalous, the scandal that is created when someone attempts to rely on emotion. This is a little what happened with *1900.* Some of the Italian intellectuals rejected *1900,* probably partly because after the success of *Last Tango in Paris* I had become physically unbearable to a lot of people, partly because *1900* was a film that made you surrender yourself to your emotions. Nowadays there is a total rejection of emotion; emotions are considered something shameful. I believe, though, that in today's world emotion is the only means of communication, emotion is really what allows us to make contact, the emotion that lies at the bottom of the well of reason.

– *From this point of view, emotion is perhaps the only means of bringing about a change in men's relationships.*

– If cinema is capable of changing anything, it is in relation to all other things. It isn't because millions of people see a film, whereas a poem is read by a few thousand, a few hundred, a few dozen people, that it can change anything. It is illusory to even think that political cinema can change anything. If we don't realize this, we are very innocent and also very guilty: to believe that after seeing a film the public is going to run to join the Communist Party, is an innocent attitude that we don't have the right to adopt. We must realize that this is not true, we must realize that cinema is complementary to any great cultural movement, or rather, to any great political movement. Cinema is nothing but one moment in this more general movement. In 1968, there were a lot of grand, marvelous and stupid things said: "The camera is like a machine gun." There were a lot of people who said this. Me too, for a moment, I also let myself be swept up by this idea. In fact, it was a romantic, juvenile and blind idea.

– *In terms of the political limitations of a film, it seems that* 1900 *is less an optimistic film, triumphalist even some have written, than a profoundly desperate film.*

– I think that *1900* is a desperately optimistic but surely not triumphalist film. I find it desperately optimistic in terms of the significance Gramsci gave to this idea. We could cite Gramsci's famous saying, though nowadays it is rather hackneyed [2]... I think there is perhaps a rather voluntary optimism in *1900*, like the one someone has who is an activist in a left-wing party and who can't help believing that the final outcome of all the common efforts of the popular masses will be victory. This is, shall we say, the optimistic side of the film, though at the same time there is also the despair of knowing that everything we are talking about is, for the moment, a dream, a utopia. And it is this, in the film, that is so very desperate.

– *Despair is something, it seems, that is common to many Italian directors.*

– *1900* would like to get beyond this despair by prefiguring a revolutionary period which, here, is still in the realm of utopia. Because of this, I was told by certain politicians: "But, after Liberation, we never put the bosses on trial." In my film, this trial against management only appears to take place in 1945; in reality it is set in the future, it's a dream. This whole sequence is anticipation, it's *the dream of something*. To understand this sequence's signif-

icance, it's enough to correctly read the film. We need to teach people how to read films because when it comes to cinema incredible illiteracy exists... especially among intellectuals. The public has no problem, they surrender to emotion. Intellectuals, however, leaving the theater believe they've understood the film since they think they've understood the movie's subject matter. There is still a "subject matterism" therefore, just as in the days of Jdanov and Stalinism. It's hopeless, and it's part of the despair in *1900*. But, on the other hand, the film is optimistic since it is conscious of tremendous communication, conscious of a great celebration of public communication, communication with the great popular masses. In Italy, it was the biggest box-office success in years. So, quantitatively, this means the most communication of all the films shown. And from a qualitative point of view?... It's a desperate film, though, because we know that few people read cinema as it should be read.

– *However, in trying to understand the climate that prevailed in Italy after the release of the film, it should be said that* 1900 *touched upon some pretty sensitive issues. For example, the relationship between Alfredo (Robert De Niro) and Attila (Donald Sutherland) brought up the difficult problem of the relationship between the bourgeoisie and Fascism.*

– If we analyze *1900* – the film has a solid foundation, it was the result of much reflection and the screenplay was carefully developed – we see that it's not Alfredo who finances Attila; it's the preceding generation that financed Fascism and which, in a certain way, invented it. Alfredo is the generation that followed and inherited Fascism, but didn't create it. Moreover, Alfredo is a very passive man, very weak. Attila and Regina (Laura Betti), the two Fascists, are not Fascism *per se*, but two *individual* Fascists. They represent all the monstruosity, all the aggressiveness the other bourgeois characters possess, but that they don't have the courage to express. Attila and Regina are representatives, as in an Elizabethan tragedy, where certain characters are truly representatives of the aggressiveness of all the others. Alfredo can't find the courage or the force to free himself from Attila until the moment

---

[2] Gramsci spoke of "the pessimism of reason and the optimism of the will."

his alter ego, Olmo (Gerard Depardieu), has left. Alfredo isn't the old Berlinghieri (Burt Lancaster) of the nineteenth century, neither is he his father, Giovanni Berlinghieri either (Romolo Valli), that man who was just as prosaic and just as devoid of style when compared to the patriarch. Alfredo is already a Dorothean[3], a Christian Democrat; he creates conflicting extremisms and, indirectly even, unconsciously even, he constantly uses Attila against Olmo, and vice versa. This is something that I've just realized right now; it had never occurred to me before. At what point does Alfredo free himself from Attila? It's when Olmo has left: in Olmo's absence, he can detach himself from Attila and dismiss him. He no longer needs anyone who serves as a filter against Olmo. Alfredo is profoundly and violently jealous of Olmo; in addition, there's a homosexual relationship between the two men which is expressed through Alfredo's jealousy. For example, in the sequence at the inn when Alfredo says to Ada (Dominique Sanda) that he smells Olmo's scent on her, there is a moment of jealous homosexual delirium. Moreover, little by little as *1900* develops, we go from a story in the style of the nineteenth-century novel to a story which instead is more influenced by psycho-analysis.

– *You mentioned that Attila wasn't Fascism "per se," but "an individual" Fascist. It would seem difficult to express this nuance, since everything in cinema becomes symbolic, each character assumes values that surpass his simple characteristics as an individual.*

– It's true that in a film everything becomes symbolic, but at the same time cinema's language is the one that resorts the least to symbols: a tree is a tree, a house is a house – this particular tree, this particular house – and Attila is Attila. This is why in *1900* I never used parts of newsreels, I never showed Fascism in general, but only the Fascism that existed in that radius of twenty kilometers comprising the estate, the village, and the next town. Moreover, I also wanted to go beyond Italian Fascism and that is why I chose Donald Sutherland rather than an Italian actor to play the part of Attila. I had first thought of using an Italian, for example, Ugo Tognazzi, who's from Cremona. Attila also comes from Cremona, the city Farinacci[4] came from, the infamous Fascist "bludgeoner." Tognazzi is a very good actor; nevertheless I thought he might have given too much naturalism to the character. I wanted Attila to be portrayed in a naturalistic way, but in addition, beyond this reading, he was to express something more than Italian Fascism, a kind of universal Fascism, the violence, the sado-masochism of Elizabethan characters. That is why I went searching for an actor who really had a particular kind of build. It's not by chance that later a famous Italian director chose him to construct a kind of... So, if we interpret the character of Attila as a metaphor for Fascism, I'd like it to be not just Fascism from 1921 to 1945, but for Fascism of all times – Fascism as a spiritual dimension, Fascism as a projection of the monster inside.

– *Your films are often the meeting point between external elements and autobiographical elements. Where is the boundary between the two?*

– It's a phenomenon that's true of anyone who expresses himself, not only in cinema, but in any form of expression. The problem is managing to find the harmony between one's own life experience and the imaginary. It's very difficult for me today to remember and draw a line in my films between what was autobiographical and what was made up, even in a recent film like *1900*.

– *Does your work with screenwriters help you to integrate the different influences we find in your films?*

– It depends. There are films I've written alone and

---

[3] An important Christian Democratic trend. This movement owed its name to the convent of Saint Dorothy where its founding politicians met.

[4] Roberto Farinacci, founder of the combat groups of Cremona and later mayor of Cremona, was one of the most violent figures in the Fascist conquest for power. In 1925, he became Secretary General of the National Fascist Party. He was shot by the partisans in 1945.

An admirable woman and an actress in the maturity of her art, Alida Valli in Bernardo Bertolucci's *Strategia del ragno/The Spider's Stratagem.*

there are films which, on the contrary, I've written with screenwriters. For example, I wrote *Before the Revolution* alone; *Partner* with Gianni Amico; *The Spider's Stratagem* with Marilù Parolini and Edoardo De Gregorio; the screenplay of *The Conformist,* though drawn from a novel by Moravia, I wrote alone; *Last Tango in Paris* was done with Kim Arcalli, and I wrote the screenplay of *1900* with my brother Giuseppe and Kim Arcalli. It was a different experience every time. Screenwriters are there to wake you up if you're sleepy, to point out things you don't see but that are often right in front of you. They also serve to give you parts of themselves thinking perhaps they're giving you others. The more I progress, the easier I find it collaborating with other people. When I first started making films, when I made *The Grim Reaper,* my experience had been in poetry and from the first day of shooting, I stopped writing, I never wrote another verse. I was coming from the very solitary and perverse experience of poetry writing; I thought films were really the works of one per-

son only, were one unique emotion, one single eye. The more I progress, I understand, especially since *1900* which was a work of collective creativity, that I have to open myself up to others. The whole myth of auteur cinema is bound up in the fear of communicating with your collaborators and especially with the public: the public, in the end, being the real collaborator of the film, the one that loves it, hates it, participates in it, surrenders to it.

– In your filmography, in terms of screenplays, we can distinguish between a period of collaboration with Gianni Amico, and a period of collaboration with Kim Arcalli. Do two periods really exist?

– I met Gianni Amico with *Before the Revolution.* There was a complicity between Gianni and I, the crazy enthusiasm of cinephiles; we thought we were taking risks and at the same time protected ourselves behind pretexts that we were being rigorous or experimenting, just to justify our refusing to try to communicate. Kim Arcalli really helped me free myself from all of this and accept dialogue. With Gianni, our work was based on elective affinities; with Kim, on the violence of our differences. Nevertheless, it would be too perfect to think that anyone has such a lot of influence over you. Instead I think we choose a certain kind of collaborator at a certain moment, and choose another kind at a time when we're ready for a change. So, in my filmography, there really is an Amico time and an Arcalli time; however, there is an intermediate stage with *The Spider's Stratagem* when there was neither one nor the other but Marilù Parolini and Edoardo De Gregorio. This film represented the first opening up after *Partner*. *Partner* was an experience I lived like an illness; it was a totally neurotic film, a sick film, schizophrenic. *1900*, on the contrary, I feel is a healthy film. To explain this we would need to get into a long, complicated, and not very interesting discussion. I would just say that *Partner* was a sick film and that, in terms of this illness, *1900* was a film that resolved certain poblems. But as far as these problems are concerned, I don't feel like saying whether I'm for or against illness or for or against health – health doesn't exist.

– Partner *was a sick film that reflected your own illness. How did you recover from that condition?*

– I came out of it gradually, from *The Spider's Stratagem*. This being said, it wasn't a coincidence that when I began that film, I also started psychoanalysis; or, better yet, a psychoanalytic career parallel to a filmmaking career.

– *Did this analysis last a long time?*

– I'm still under analysis. That means it's been almost eight years that I've been under analysis. Nevertheless, it's a strange kind of analysis that stops every time I make a film. Duirng the time I'm shooting, the film replaces analysis. I see the end of this analysis as something very distant.

– *To go back to your collaborators, it's interesting to note that Kim Arcalli was both screenwriter and editor of your most recent films, two activities that rarely go together.*

– Arcalli is the one who managed to get me to ac-

cept editing. Until *Partner,* and even up to *The Spider's Stratagem*, I had refused or, in one way or another, even brushed aside the moment of editing. During those years, those wonderful sixties, I had theories on cinema, I considered editing a banal phase, the time when things are organized, when order is put into the marvelous chaos of rushes all out of order. I was really against editing. Then, little by little, with Kim, there was a long conflict and he made me realize that the footage shot is much richer than we think. This all came from auteur cinema strategy; basically the author said: "The way I write, I shoot; I edit only as a result of the way I filmed." However now, instead, I edit even against the way I've shot. The change in my attitude towards editing was something very important. Naturally, it wasn't only a question of technique, it was also a question of what I considered a profound change. And then, Kim is such a stimulating person, so full of ideas. With him, collaborating goes beyond what is usually involved in editing a film. At the editing stage, a revision of the screenplay occurs almost always, based on the footage you've shot. This happened the first time we worked together, that is, when we edited *The Conformist*. After that, I also wanted him as screenwriter, and we made *Last Tango in Paris* and *1900* together.

– *Arcalli never wrote any screenplays with any other directors except you, did he?*

– Perhaps he did once for Tinto Brass' first film, *Chi lavora è perduto*. But that was a film they really made together, I think; Arcalli even had a part in the movie; he played a veteran partisan who went mad and was interned in an asylum.

– *In his* Scritti corsari, *Pasolini shows that the consumer society is a form of Fascism that leads to the destruction of all other cultures.*

– In a way I made *1900* in order to strike up a dialogue with Pasolini on the subject. I wanted to show him that in Emilia, as if by some miracle, the phenomenon hadn't occurred. On this island – let's call it an island since all around it Italy has changed a lot – the farmers have managed to maintain the ancient culture of their origins. When Pasolini spoke of cul-

Jean-Louis Trintignant and Dominique Sanda in Bertolucci's *Il conformista/The Conformist*.

tural destruction and standardization, he was thinking of the south of Italy, of the outskirts of Rome, and big cities. However in Emilia, socialism, and then communism, made farmers truly realize that their culture was a great treasure, and the destruction which Pasolini refers to didn't occur. This was thanks to communism: in southern Italy, however, the left is very weak. It's a paradox, but in Emilia, Marxism helped to preserve cultural origins. So, with *1900* I wanted to respond to Pasolini and involve him in a dialogue on this particular theme. His view was very apocalyptic and I wanted to focus on more everyday considerations. I wanted to show him that I had found hundreds of faces that weren't faces that had been blighted, made commonplace by consumer society, but faces that had remained the same as the ones I remember when I was eight years old, the same faces that existed before the war. In short, I wanted to show him that the peasant farmers of Emilia – somewhat as in China – had become aware of the great treasure their culture represented.

– *Does living in Rome make you feel uprooted?*

– In a way no, since I've lived in Rome since I was eleven and it's been my home for many years.

Nevertheless, I've always considered Rome an unbearable city; it's a city of appearances, a city where work is impossible, you can never get anything started, you sleep all the time. It's a city where it's good to edit, which is a rather digestive activity. And this is why I've shot very little in Rome: *The Grim Reaper,* some of *Partner,* a few scenes for *The Conformist*. Rome is a city where you can't even go to the movies; everything is dubbed, even *1900* was. You get the impression that if you film the city, nothing will remain imprinted on the film. Rome is going through an awful period. Paris is worse. Of course, you can see more films there, but the weight of the French bourgeoisie is terrible. This bourgeoisie, which at one time had made a revolution, is so arrogant, hard, tyrannical, that you can even feel it physically. The Italian bourgeoisie is more vulnerable and less solid, less powerful, less historical in some ways. In Italy you feel more vitality, though at the same time it seems to me that, in these past months, it's becoming more and more difficult to live here, particularly in Rome. I don't think this is a problem specific to Italy; it's the same all over Europe, we're living a period of transition, a period without style.

The rages of history, Fascist Attila (Donald Sutherland) against Communist peasant farmers in Bernardo Bertolucci's *1900.*

– The problem of identity is often evoked in your films.

– To go back to the question before, in certain ways I was uprooted, pulled out of the region where I was born. My family moved from the countryside to the big city, six hours away by train: everything that had existed, no longer existed; I had lost my reference points. The first few years, I rejected that city. So, concerning identity I think I had, and perhaps continue to have, great problems. A theme that returns constantly in all of my films, is the theme of the double, the theme of schizophrenia. In *Partner,* the theme of schizophrenia is faced openly. In *1900,* it's the same, the two heroes are born on the same day and represent two different classes. In a certain way, they are two sides of the same person. In *The Spider's Stratagem,* the father and the son are played by the same actor: Giulio Brogi only changes his jacket and shoes, but everything else stays the same. The problem of the double is a double problem, so great I really don't know what to say. All I know is that it always comes back in my films, perhaps the last time will be *1900.*

– Can you explain what it means to you to be a member of the Italian Communist Party?

– Looking back, first of all I can explain in more detail why I joined the Communist Party. In a way, I've always been a Communist. In the beginning it was for sentimental reasons. It all began when I was a child living in the countryside. Try to imagine, on a small scale, a Berlinghieri family and a Dalco family: a microscopic situation compared to the dimensions of these two families in *1900* – on the one hand, a middle-class or petty bourgeois agricultural family, and on the other, a family of farmers that consisted of ten members instead of forty as in the film. Naturally I spent my childhood years almost always in the peasant farmers' houses: all bosses' children love to be with the farmers' families. I spoke of sentimental reasons because the word communist was a word I often heard from the farmers. I learned one day that "communist" meant "hero" when the farmers were talking about a demonstration organized following the death of a young man, who had been killed by the police, and whose name was Alberti. That was in 1949-1950, during a period of big strikes. I remember that we were in a tomato field, the women were picking tomatoes, bent over the plants that were quite low. I asked who Alberti was. And then, Nella, who was one of the peasant farmers, raised her body up to the height of my eight years; I saw this body rising, I saw this face with a straw hat look at me and say, after a pause of silence like that of a great actress: "Alberti is a Communist." From that moment on, of course, I had become a Communist. Under those circumstances, with that pause, with that light, with the fact that Alberti had been killed by the "Celere"[5], anyone would have. So that's the real archaeology of my communism. I have been a Communist since that day and I never had any doubts about it. I should mention that doubts always come to me from inside. Doubts never come from outside factors; I have great respect for out-

---

[5] The "Celere" ("Rapid") was the official riot squad.

side factors, for external reality. Thus I have never had any doubt about Communism, even if I didn't join the Party immediately.

– What made you join the Party?

– In an imaginary way, I was a Communist since childhood. In the early sixties the Communist Party began to worry me somewhat, a fear which I expressed in *Before the Revolution*. When the film was shown in Paris in early 1968, it was very successful; it ran in a cinema in the Latin Quarter and the number of people who went to see it was tremendous for a little art-theater film.

Before the Revolution was well received because this film, made in 1963-1964, expressed fears concerning the Communist Party which were later to be those expressed in '68. In Italy people found the film irritating, since it was rather before its time, I think coming before a series of social demands that

The isolation of Fabrizio (Francesco Barilli) at the Festa dell'Unità in *Prima della rivoluzione/Before the Revolution*.

appeared later. In 1968, when the student movement that protested against leftist parties and particularly the Communist Party was born, I felt around me such a violent anti-communist feeling that I immediately joined the C.P.

When I made *Before the Revolution,* I wanted to express the conflict in a provincial bourgeois youth, full of intellectual ambitions, in his education, his cultural background and the idealistic vision he had of the Communist Party. So I wanted to express what the reality of the Communist Party was during those years. The beginning of the sixties was a transition period between the mythical, Stalinist years of the postwar and what would later be the Berlinguer period. These were really the years that later would kill Togliatti[6]. During this period, the Italian Communist Party rather lacked style. I think Fabrizio in *Before the Revolution* reproached the Communist Party above all for its lack of style. All in all, I'd like to say that I'm not very political, I never was, at least not the way most people are today. Whatever the case may be, during those years I wasn't yet a member of the Party. In 1968, the year that *Before the Revolution* was so successful in Paris, in May there was a great explosion of anti-communist feeling, in the midst of many other exalting things. I think we all needed 1968 even if in an attempt to present a political stand this was one of the first signs of the way the bourgeoisie would try to evade, to camouflage its anti-communist feeling. This anti-communism of obvious bourgeois origins continued. I felt it around me particularly among the young but also among the less young, among those who had rediscovered a second youth in embracing the movement of '68. This is what prompted me to join the Party. In 1969 I couldn't stand that anti-communism any longer. At that point, I told myself, for reasons of honesty, coherence, loyalty when it came to the Party and to my Communist comrades, I had

[6] Palmiro Togliatti died in 1964.

[7] Bertolucci is alluding here to a meeting which was to be held at the University of Rome the day after the interview, a meeting which caused, after union leader Lama's speech, serious confrontations and the closing of the University.

to join. So I've been a member of the Party since then.

– *I find* Before the Revolution *a film that remains vital even today.*

– Indeed, when the '68 phenomenon broke out, it seemed to me that everything happening was already déjà vu, already seen, already heard – of course in a general way. It was a little like a repeat of what *Before the Revolution* had said, a repeat of the relationship shown between the Communist Party and a young bourgeois youth's sentimental and cultural background, which was also true of the 1968 students. That night I listened to one of the free radio stations, one of the radio stations that used to say, "what I mean is..." every five seconds. It was about the occupation of the universities, about Luciano Lama, the secretary of the C.G.I.L. who was going to speak at the university of Rome[7], about the government finding support in the Communists' abstention. It was a juvenile discussion, politically zero, about Communists who had left the opposition and were supporting the government by abstaining. They had understood nothing of Berlinguer's speech on austerity, a brilliant speech. From time to time, Berlinguer had extraordinary intuitions: he transformed the meaning of the word austerity, he called austerity a great revolutionary arm to change the model of society. The expropriations that the leftists proposed concerned consumer goods. Thus, they refused to understand and admit that from then on the consumer age was over and would never be recovered. It was going to be very hard for them once they discovered that being better off didn't mean going backwards to a model of living, or society, that was maintained and still existed then but that tomorrow would disappear. Being better off meant advancing towards something that was perhaps less comfortable, but that nevertheless could transform everything and, above all, the economic relationships between individuals.

– *What is the relationship between your work as filmmaker and the fact that you're a Communist?*

– It's only with great difficulty that I manage to de-

Il Quarto Stato, the famous painting by of Giuseppe Pellizza da Volpedo that is a backdrop for the film credits of *Novecento/1900*.

scribe in a linear way my relationship with the Communist Party. It's a relationship that, during *1900,* was at its most intense, be it in terms of what I had imagined, or in terms of the possible reaction of the Communist Party to the film, or in terms of what was later the real reaction. Basically, there's a great feeling of guilt in me as an individual, as an activist, towards the Party: I feel I don't go to the branch I belong to enough, I'm not involved enough in the branch's activities, and a Party member should be truly active in his branch. On the other hand, I feel however, that I was an activist when I made *1900,* even if *1900* was a film that was almost like a dream, built and structured as if in a dream, on the scale of the one dreaming it, that is, the public. I find that the quarrel that was partially sparked – of course in a minor way compared to what I would have hoped, and in terms of what I had tried to cause within the Communist cultural world, for the most part rejected – was quite an important quarrel.

I find there's a big discrepancy between the intuition Berlinguer expresses, this very great philosopher and poet, and all the apparatus, the exterior armour of the Party, a very bureaucratic apparatus and one which is apparently very anti-Berlinguerian – but perhaps these are Berlinguer's two souls. In fact, I have never really expressed any views on this, so I don't have a ready answer. I thought *1900* was a Communist film and I still think so, a Communist film, first of all, because it is a film in sync with the Communist Party line of the entire postwar period, from Togliatti right up to Berlinguer. It's a film that accepts and is part of a mode of production, that of big capital, precisely in order to emphasize the contradictions the filmmaker is up against; this is already of great importance, even if some people, in a rather simplistic way, have accused me of wanting to make *1900* into a model. It's exactly the opposite – *1900* is an exception. Not me nor anyone else could ever reproduce an experience of that kind. It's an exception precisely because it's a film that destroys itself, a film that, as a mode of production, is an explosion. *1900* is truly a symptom of a specific period, absolutely not a model. Everything that was often said against the seminar organized on *1900* at the Venice Biennial last year is very wrong: the Biennial, in organizing a seminar on the film, was accused of wanting to hold up *1900* as a model. I think it's exactly the opposite: *1900* is a unique film, not an example.

To bring up another aspect, in *1900* I was looking for a harmony, perhaps impossible to find, between Marx and Freud. It isn't a film of historical compromise... not a film on historical compromise, but a film that, in cinema, *is* historical compromise. I accord historical compromise – you have to read these remarks in a surreal way just like I'm saying them in a rather surreal way – a highly esteemed significance, since in my opinion this is the most important thing that has appeared in politics in this country over the past years, the most important thing, along with Berlinguer's speech on austerity, a speech that was the object of ambiguities and was even misunderstood within the Communist Party. For this reason, the speech wasn't recognized as being as important as it was. *1900* is historical compromise even if some might be surprised that I combine the film, and the historical compromise. For

me historical compromise means what I was saying before, that is, the possibility even for someone from a bourgeois background – as have been many worthy men in the history of the Communist Party – to find a point where his culture can be put to use to serve the masses.

– *Many of your films bring moments of Italian history to the screen. Can you explain the kind of relationship you have with history?*

– Even if history is very important, I wouldn't call my films historical films, at least in the way history is considered by historians, or even by Marxist historians. In fact, it has been precisely the work of historians that have allowed me to deal with history in a special way. I use history, but I don't make historical films, I make films that are falsely historical because, in fact, it isn't possible to create history with the cinematic mode of expression: cinema knows only one conjugation, the present tense. This already tremendously limits the possibility of making history. *The Spider's Stratagem, The Conformist, 1900,* aren't historical films; they are films that seek to "historicize" the present. All of my films are films about the present, even when they are about the beginning of the century, the twenties or the birth of Fascism.

Bernardo Bertolucci, "first emperor" of Italian cinema, on the set of *L'ultimo imperatore/The Last Emperor*.

Bertolucci on the set of *Novecento/1900* with Francesca Bertini, legendary star of silent movies.

– *The theme of Fascism as a period in Italy's history appears often in your films.*

– To talk about Fascism means to talk about the present. In *1900* I had dealt with the problem of the birth of Fascism as a historian – and because of this, historians complained a little about the way I had presented things – I should have shown a whole series of stages in the relationships that developed between the ruling class and the nationalists and the interventionists, who were powerless after the war. Instead, I tried to synthesize the birth of Fascism in two sequences: one, when the owners, in church, take up a collection to pay the Fascists, and the other, when a tailor sews a black shirt on Attila's body. In my opinion these are – and this is strange – the two most Brechtian scenes in the film. I felt that, in one way or another, I had to show the birth of Fascism; I preferred to resort to a Brechtian type ellipsis instead of showing it in a naturalistic way, as in all historical Italian cinema.

– *There is also in almost all of your films a relationship with memory, notably in* The Spider's Stratagem *and in* Last Tango in Paris, *where a young woman practically devoid of memory, without a past, meets a man who entirely consists of memory.*

– Yes, in *Last Tango in Paris* Marlon Brando is really the material of living memory; he is made of memory. On the other hand, Maria Schneider is devoid of memory; and so she can calmly walk over the corpse of this man, and she does this throughout the whole film, with a supreme innocence and unconscious cruelty. In my opinion, the film is political because it's a film about confrontation, about a power struggle between a character who has no past – and then we discover that Maria does in fact have one, since the weapon she uses to kill Brando is after all a gun that belonged to her father who had been a *pied-noir* officer – and a character who, on the contrary, is made of memory, of the past, of cinematographic and literary memory. Basically, Brando resembles in a way Minnelli's and Miller's characters; he's halfway between the Gene Kelly in *An American in Paris* and the *Tropics* characters living in Paris. In fact, at first I wanted to call the film *An American in Paris 2*.

– *When you choose your actors, you use actors of very diverse ancestries, foreign actors, actors who are almost beginners, actors associated with the history of Italian cinema such as Francesca Bertini, Tino Scotti, Massimo Girotti, Alida Valli, Yvonne Sanson. What is this choice based on?*

– When I don't know the actors, I choose them based on immediate impressions, the first sensations I get when we meet. I decide to choose an actor in the first two minutes after meeting him. This is what happened, for example, with Robert De Niro and Gérard Depardieu. In the other cases, actors with a long past behind them are like living citations, citations of perhaps nothing particular; nevertheless, if we take a closer look, there is probably a reason, a justification, for example, choosing Yvonne Sanson to play the role of Stefania Sandrelli's mother in *The Conformist*: even if Yvonne Sanson's films, *Nobody's Child, L'angelo bianco,* etc., came after Fascism, they nevertheless express a whole petty-bourgeois mythology.

– *When Massimo Girotti works out in* Last Tango in Paris, *we can't help thinking of the athletic actor who played in* The Iron Crown.

– In *Last Tango in Paris* I had thought of putting Marlon Brando and Massimo Girotti face to face. They were both very handsome when they had been young. One became an international monument and the other, on the contrary, stayed more provincial, though enjoying his own poetic quality which *Ossessione* and perhaps *The Iron Crown* had given him, and also by the fact that he never became a big star. The idea of putting them face to face had perhaps something rather sadistic about it, but nevertheless they are both great professionals. And then, I liked it because Girotti has less stomach and more hair than Brando; it was a little like Girotti

taking revenge on Marlon Brando. At the same time, I think that Girotti did everything with self-irony. Here again there was the theme of the double; Girotti was Brando's double, they both had identical bathrobes. Francesca Bertini in *1900* was truly the beginning of the century. There was a scene in which she grasps at a curtain, the same as in her silent films. Unfortunately, the scene didn't fit in with the economy of the film and it was cut during editing; the homage was too obvious. Tino Scotti, Alida Valli were also living citations.

– *The choice of foreign actors, for example, a French woman and an American man as heroes of* Last Tango in Paris, *emphasizes your search for a culture that's not exclusively Italian, your attraction for a kind of cultural cosmopolitanism.*

– In this area, as in the others, I have always acted according to the principle of contradiction or, if you like, of dialectic. I think I'm very Italian and even, if it exists, very Emilian. I was brought up in a family in which culture was really the world of freedom. At home you could read everything. But it was most especially cinema that gave me the most international part of my personality, of my culture. I loved cinema, a love which perhaps I no longer feel; it has become so difficult, particularly in Rome, to see good films. To love someone or something, you have to see them, meet from time to time.

– *Your cultural cosmopolitanism is perhaps an attempt to bring Italian culture out of a kind of provincialism that characterizes it in some of its expressions.*

– This is perhaps a result of my work, certainly not what I try to do originally. It's an effect of my way of working or the nature of my films. At home, remember, there were a lot of books and I always lived literature and especially poetry, not as something specific; national or local, but as something general, a little as if all the poems of all the poets were one unique poem. Basically now I think that all films form one unique great film, which is cinema. It is in this perspective that the contradiction between the fact of locating my films as precisely

On the set of *L'ultimo imperatore/The Last Emperor.*

as possible and the fact of being as open as possible should be understood. To be open to what you call cultural cosmopolitanism means to love all kinds of different things very much, for example, many filmmakers from many different countries. There's nothing that can make you want to make a film more than seeing beautiful films. Seeing beautiful films is the most stimulating thing there is. So I really feel that film schools are useless; lessons of style, directing, diction, serve no purpose. What's important for a film director in a school of cinema is to see films, lots of films. This is why Langlois is the greatest master of cinema ever, because he showed six, eight films a day.

(SECOND INTERVIEW)

– *After a rather exotic parenthesis, if we can call it that, what prompted your return to Italy with* Stealing Beauty?

– I've always felt that I left Italy during a time when I didn't like it. Personally, I had the feeling that the eighties were "dirty," very corrupt, very cynical. I couldn't stand filming in Italy any longer. I was quite disconcerted by my lack of will, desire, to shoot in Italy. So I went away as far as possible, in search of something very different. I first tried fulfilling my impossible dream, to make *Red Harvest* by Dashiell Hammett in the United States, and I lost a year or two on this project. And then a strange coincidence happened. MGM sent me the screenplay for *The Human Condition* whose rights it owned for another year. And almost simultaneously someone gave me to read what was claimed to be the autobiography of Pu Yi, the last emperor of China. So I said, "OK, I'm going to China." The friend who had given me the emperor's autobiography knew China a little since he had worked on *Marco Polo* [1]. And so I said to Mark Peploe and Enzo Ungari, "Come with me. The four of us are going to China for a month." All of them had read the autobiography, *From Emperor to Citizen*. I was pretty determined, I must say, since this project was like a lifesaver for me: it was already three years since I had no longer made a film. And just like that, I found myself by chance (but in fact I don't really believe in chance), in China, and then in Africa, and finally in Nepal. And the last time in Boutang, was also the beginning, in Milan, of the "Clean Hands" operation. I said to myself, "What luck! The country can now take stock of its conscience a little, collectively reflect on this mentality in Italy that has existed since the ancient Romans: bureaucracy and corruption. We're lucky that we can change." Of course there was Craxi, and some corrupt politicans, but mc too, like everyone else, I had given 50,000 lire to hurry up a passport procedure, or 10,000 lire for someone to watch my car triple parked. All of that was endemic. So then I hadn't been wrong, in the early eighties, when I had discerned the corruption that would explode in the early nineties. And I told myself, "Things are going to change and, anyway, I'm fed up: I want to go back to Italy!" But I had never really left Italy. I lived for some time in London and I'm there a lot since my wife has a house there, but I've always had a place in Rome. I wanted to make a sequel to *1900*. However, after I found myself in that void after making *Little Buddha,* I felt it wasn't the right time yet for a sequel to *1900*: I had to learn how to see Italy again, learn how to film it again. I wanted to do something where Italy would only be a backdrop, where Italy would be seen through the eyes of foreigners, something that would be based on the beauty of Italy. I wasn't

ready to confront the reality of Italy: so I disguised myself as an Anglo-Saxon cultural tourist, like the many you find in the Chianti area. Also, I really wanted to make a production smaller than the three previous ones. There was this house that belonged to one of my friends, a sculptor whose works you see in the film. That's how I got this idea about the fantasies surrounding a young girl: she's there because she's decided that she has a mission, she wants to lose her virginity. Of course, in the rather cosmopolitan atmosphere of the house, this creates some shivers. But it was a fantasy. I needed a girl who wasn't Italian, not even European, since it had to be as if she were parachuted in there, someone who would have no ties, no roots, but in the end discovers that she in fact does. Since it was the story of a girl, I needed a woman to write it with me. I thought of an American. A female friend suggested Susan Minot, whom she knew. I met Susan. It was then that I really discovered what it meant to be a cinema buff. And we got to work right away. I told her the story, she started writing. We worked a lot together, we made several versions of the screenplay.

– *Was it the distance you felt from an Italy which you no longer considered your own that prompted you, then, not to work with Vittorio Storaro, who had been your chief cameraman for a long time?*

– During *Little Buddha* we decided that it would be good to take a little vacation one from the other. I think it's absolutely normal. However, in fact, that had only happened once, a few years before, when I made *The Tragedy of a Ridiculous Man* with Carlo Di Palma. You know, Vittorio and I are a couple older than my wife and I (and I've been married for twenty-two years). So, sometimes you get the feeling that if you work with someone else, it's a separation and separation is like death... When I was shooting *The Tragedy of a Ridiculous Man,* Vittorio was making a film with someone else. I felt that that separation was also a choice on his part. I wanted very, very sharp photography. Vittorio never gets very sharp since his way of lighting comes from a school that uses very little light; even if the set's facilities are tremendous, it

---

[1] A television superpoduction.

seems as if there is very little light. The film was about the complete fog that covers up the question of terrorism in Italy: nothing was understood by anyone. A very foggy story. I thought that it was necessary to counterbalance this by an extremely well-defined image.

– *You wanted to recreate the same sensation in* Stealing Beauty.

– It was a film about a young girl. I thought it would be very difficult, that it would be a challenge, a real bet against the odds for me to try to put myself in the shoes of a young girl. I therefore also needed someone young for photography. And Darius Khondji was young. What was strange was that I had always called Vittorio "the Persian prince," because of the color of his skin and his rather exotic, oriental face, and I found another Persian...

– *How did you choose him?*

– I started looking around. I also liked Piotr Sobocinski a lot, who had worked on *Red,* which was very beautiful work. I had seen what Darius had done on *Before the Rain* and *Delicatessen.* And I met him. What I liked was that he was like Vittorio when we had made *The Conformist* and *The Spider's Stratagem.* He had the same kind of enthusiasm, the fever, the obsessional character that I had known how to put to use and that had inspired me for a long time. He was also someone who had experience in television, advertising, video clips. And from the beginning, precisely because I wanted a change, I was aiming for lightness. It was something that obsessed me about this film. I wanted to do something quite light, which doesn't mean superficial, but... I listened a lot to Mozart. In that dimension, I wanted something that gave me the idea of chamber music rather than a big orchestra.

– Stealing Beauty *is a very intimist film in this way. It was the first time, though, that you used the wide screen for an intimist story.*

– That was something Darius and I decided together. Until then, Darius had never made a big-budget film except for *La cité des enfants perdus* on which he had worked in the beginning. His image of me was an "epic" format, the scope. In fact, I had only shot once in real cinemascope, in *The Last Emperor:* for *Little Buddha,* the ancient historical parts were shot in 65mm. I didn't want to immediately discourage this guy by saying, "No, that's not at all what I want to do." So after all, I thought, why not? It was a good way to counterbalance the lightness. It was a way of balancing out an excess of lightness. I was afraid the film might just unexpectedly take off, being so light. And then with Gianni Silvestri, my set designer, we had decided to choose strong colors. We took red earth from a neighboring quarry to give that color to the road that leads to the house. I wanted the green of the vineyards, the red of the earth. Once again, to give weight. I was always afraid of not having enough weight. And we studied the Fauves a lot: we studied Matisse, Derain, whose trees were red.

– *And those frequent references to Siena in the background.*

– Yes, in the distance. It was like the mirage of something one had rejected. At the same time, Siena, seen from the hills of Chianti, isn't very different from the Siena of Simone Martini, in fourteenth- and fifteenth-century painting. I always try to establish a relationship with the art of the place I'm filming. When I went to China, I spent weeks meeting young Chinese film directors. Chen Kaige had just made his first film, *Yellow Land,* and I asked him to act in *The Last Emperor.* I wanted to get to know Chinese cinema: not only things that had already been done, but the cinema still to be made. In the same way, for me, Siena was the painting of the fourteenth and fifteenth centuries. There were many things in the screenplay that completely disappeared from the film later on. There was a reproduction in the young girl's newspaper at the beginning, of which part reappears on the door of her room. It's a painting by an artist who was called *Il maestro dell'osservanza* [the master of observation, *Trans.*]. Very symbolic: there was a woman saint, a dog with a human arm in his mouth and the plains which looked like a tiled floor. I used Siena as a reference, but also the rejection of the city. Towards the end of the shooting, I finally decided to enter the city for the credits of the film.

– We get the impression that you were constantly afraid of the lightness of this film. Stealing Beauty *is striking because of its luminous quality but, at the same time, there are some obscure areas in the screenplay. Notably the father's search, which is extremely mysterious. I'm thinking in particular about the credits, when the heroine, asleep, is filmed by a man whom we see nothing of except a bracelet and later on, thanks to this bracelet, we discover that the person was Carlo. And this makes us wonder who the real father was and if the matter has truly been resolved as Lucy believes. We wonder if even the cassette itself won't play some role later on.*

– You're right. This was something that, right up to the last minutes of editing, had an explanation. When everyone, except the sculptor, went to the reception, Daisy searched through the house and stole a cassette. She watched it and we saw the beginning of the film, a minute of terrifying images of Sarajevo. Images never shown on TV before, that a buddy of mine had given me. She watched all of this like a child watches TV, that is, expressionless. On the same cassette there were two things that ran one into the other. For moral reasons, I didn't want to exploit anything so tragic. Really, it made you dizzy. It was like when I had made *La luna*. The guy in the film goes to a bar and Franco Citti was there. The young man was dancing a little like Travolta; it was the rage at the time. And then Citti kissed him and asked him to dance with him. The guy was shooting off, and then he woke up. He had been asleep in front of the TV where he sees the death of Pier Paolo [Pasolini, *Trans.*]. He looked around him and those watching the TV were all the pimps whom I had known when I was an assistant for Pier Paolo on *Accattone*. Fifteen or sixteen years later, the pimps were

Io ballo da sola/Stealing Beauty (Liv Tyler).

watching Pasolini's death. We find a little bit of this in Marco Tullio Giordana's film [2]. And there again, I had an excess of puritanism: I can't talk about things like that, that are so horrible. I remember that Franco was supposed to cry. He couldn't. So he asked for some menthol. And they put in too much. All of a sudden he screamed: "I can't see anymore! ... I'm blind!" We were deep in Oedipus! [laughing].

– *I think it's good, in a story like that, that some things are left suspended. For example, why were all of those people together? What ties did they really have in common?*

– I myself spent a long time in a house like that in Tuscany. And it was only the friendship of all of those present for the host that bound them. They were all more or less intellectuals, but not exclusively. With the exception of Jean Marais, their age also made them feel close. Jean Marais evoked Cocteau. I've always liked having "ghosts" in cinema. This is one of my vices. It's cinema. I also like generation gaps: for young people, grown-ups are old. But for grown-ups, Jean Marais was the old man.

– *What made you choose the music?*

– It was a way of identifying the girl. It's the music that the girl listens to. I listened a lot to music during the filming and I often asked Liv what she liked. She comes from a family of performers. She's the girlfriend of one of the leaders of the band Aerosmith. What's more, when she read the screenplay, she said to me, "It's incredible! It's like my life!" It was only at the age of nine that she had learned that the man she thought was her father, wasn't really him. She met her real father then. To go back to the music, I wanted the music that young people listen to today, but I also wanted Mozart, Billie Holiday, and it was Richard Hartley who was supposed to "bridge" all of that. A lot of references, and little original music. We kept at least half of the music that we had as background music on the set for the film. The first title of the film was

Dancing by Myself. The Italian title, *Io ballo da sola* was in fact the Italian title since *Stealing Beauty* was very difficult to translate: it's at the same time the thief of beauty and beauty that steals. It's quite complex. The literal translation was pretty, but it didn't have that ambiguity. The music and the dancing were already very much present at the conception, from the writing stage: with Susan, we discussed it a lot.

– *The heroine is also death, a little. Jeremy Irons dies upon contact with her.*

– I hadn't thought of that. But it's true that this is a character who, in apprenticeship, discovers on the one hand, love and on the other, death. This is what I had in mind.

– *But we can also see her as an angel of death.*

– A little like in *Theoreme*. It's true that I was thinking a lot of *Theoreme*. But in Pasolini's film, Terence Stamp seduces everyone, and everyone changes. Here too, they change, but not ideologically. *Theoreme* was made in 1968... What was conscious in the film was that the dying writer received an injection of life, of vitality, in contact with this young girl. He follows the whole story. He's in love with her, even if it's an impossible love, even unthinkable... To stop this kind of impulse that she has started, the young girl takes the young man home all the while knowing she's not going to do anything with him. Then she goes to see Alex and, and this is one of the things I like most about Jeremy Irons' performance, he's overcome by a kind of fit of agitation, jealousy. She spends the night with the young man, but everyone in the house makes love except her. And in the morning, when she wakes up, Jeremy Irons is finished. It's the idea of the girl's virginity that gives her this ultimate vitality. And the idea of the loss of virginity that kills him.

– *Was this agitation that you just mentioned something that Jeremy Irons suggested, or did the idea come from you?*

– It was my idea. Actors always contribute something to all of my films. But this wasn't the case

---

[2] *Pasolini, un delitto italiano.*

A venomous story for a mythic actor transferred to the streets of Paris, Marlon Brando in Bernardo Bertolucci's *Ultimo tango a Parigi/Last Tango in Paris.*

here. I even asked him, in order for us to be able to feel the agitation even more, to pretend to be looking for something. He made up, of course, "This is the most beautiful thing I've ever written. Since I can't find it, it's certainly the most beautiful...."

– *For a long time, from* Last Tango in Paris, *the character who leads us into the film is often an anglo-saxon. Why?*

– I'd like to make a confession. The hero of *Last Tango in Paris* could well have been Alain Delon, Jean-Paul Belmondo or Jean-Louis Trintignant. Belmondo said to me, "This is porn, I'll never do it." Alain Delon also wanted to be producer and I thought that it was too dangerous to have the leading actor also be the producer, especially for such a sensitive film. Jean-Louis Trintignant didn't want to appear in the nude. Thanks to them, I was able to get Marlon Brando. In the end I happened upon him by chance. And I discovered the pleasure of shooting in English dialogue. The problem of all Italian films, even the most beautiful ones, even the ones I adore like Michelangelo Antonioni's, including my own films, are the dialogues. I have a tremendous problem shooting the dialogues. *Stealing Beauty* gave me a real shock when I shot a scene between two people speaking Italian. I was even tempted to have the two brothers speak English to each other. When the Italian language is acted, there's something, I can't put my finger on it... Which is why what is most beautiful in Italian theater is in dialect: Goldoni, De Filippo, Pier Paolo. Italian language seems anti-dramatic. It's a literary language, a written language. Some people, with a rather innocent malice, think that films shot in English have a bigger market. But it isn't a question of that for me.

Giuseppe Tornatore

– *Was the screenplay of* The Star Man *based on true fact? Did the character of the cameraman going around getting screen tests in the film actually exist?*

– That kind of thing really happened. And not just once. An old friend of mine told me that when he was young he had auditioned for a man looking for new actors with his camera. They had made a few screen tests but he never knew what became of those films. This was a story I had heard. Then, by investigating and researching, I discovered that these people really had existed. Of course, I don't know if they were crooks as in the story I made up...

But that there were these talent scouts – it seems, in fact, that they asked for very little money – that we know is true. Afterwards, I developed this idea a little and made the character into a crook.

It was necessary to do this since the film's main theme was the eternal impossibility of telling Sicily's story. Though there have been many tales about this region, really a very great number, sometimes almost *ad nauseam*, Sicilians, but not only they, are under the impression that Sicily's story has never been told right down to its depths.

As if there were something in Sicily's essence that couldn't be expressed by any means of communication. And so I began with the idea of a swindler who uses film that is blank and which records nothing.

– *Nevertheless, the cassette records the voices.*

– Yes, because if you think about it, in my films my characters always live an intense experience from which they often come out losers. Yet something always remains as a testimony of their experience. Totò, for example, in *Cinema Paradiso* is left only with the kisses in his films; Matteo Scuro in *Everybody's Fine* is left with photos from his life; Joe Morelli in *The Star Man* is left with the voices of those people who involuntarily helped make him better.

The crook, Joe Morelli, who leaves Sicily at the end of the film, isn't the same man he was in the beginning, when he arrived on the island.

– *What was Fabio Rinaudo's role, who appears in the credits as co-screenwriter?*

– Rinaudo was Franco Cristaldo's right-hand man for almost forty years. Rinaudo was above all a journalist, and remained so, but for several years he worked as Cristaldi's secretary and his speciality was reading screenplays. He also worked on some as co-screenwriter. For example, I believe he worked on *Murmur of the Heart* by Louis Malle, which was co-produced with Franco Cristaldi. I met him during the making of *Cinema Paradiso*, and when I made *The Star Man,* a film I had decided to make right after *Una pura formalità,* Rinaudo had left Cristaldi Films since Cristaldi had died.

I got the feeling that he suffered from no longer having good opportunities to make movies, and so I got him interested in my project.

He is a very generous man. If you describe a sensation, an idea to him, and you ask him to write a few notes, he brings you forty pages. And so, he helped me to write this screenplay very joyfully and also, if you may, somewhat hastily. Perhaps you can tell this in the film. It was a pleasant experience.

– *But the general direction of the film was completely yours?*

– Yes, of course. The screenplay, too. We had meetings. We discussed it together. Then we divided up the scenes, mine and his. And he made a rough draft as best he could. But the final rewriting of the film, I did all on my own. Nevertheless, it was a collaboration that helped me to get the film together in a very short time. It was the first time I happened to make a film back to back with another.

– *Was that an idea that came from the production department?*

Giuseppe Tornatore makes his directorial debut with a film based upon a *camorra* boss who even operates from prison. Ben Gazzara in *Il camorrista*.

– No, it came from me. When I returned from Cannes in 1994 after the presentation of *Una pura formalità;* it had been such a humiliating experience for me and so painful that I wanted to throw myself into a new film right away. I told myself that if I didn't make another film immediately, I felt that I wouldn't make another for a long time.

I wanted to make another movie right away because I had finally realized that in this profession the only moments of happiness are those when I'm writing a screenplay, preparing a film, while I'm shooting, while I'm editing. All the rest is never very much fun.

– *Was it also after the failure of* Una pura formalità *that you felt the need to return to Sicily?*

– Yes, it was something instinctive. I wanted to make a film right away, and so I had to find an idea that gave me a lot of freedom. Don't forget that *The Star Man* was finished in truly record time. Between the moment I started writing until I fin-

ished the mixing, eight and a half months elapsed. I literally threw myself into the film as if I had a rock around my neck. And that was a tremendously exalting experience.

I was truly happy. And I realized that the beautiful side of this profession was making movies. That was it. Today, I feel I'd like to repeat that experience. Because it's really true: nothing else can give you the immense energy that making a movie does.

– *How was the problem of finding locations for the shooting handled?*

– The film was shot all over Sicily, in particular, in Ragusa. There's also a scene that wasn't filmed in Sicily but in Matera in Basilicata, since in Sicily I hadn't found a place where I could shoot at 360° for that long sequence shot; and so we looked elsewhere. You can't tell. It's not a problem since it blends in with the other locations. I already knew some of the places before. And while writing the screenplay, I referred to them directly.

For other locations, I sent people to search while I was writing. Once the shot was set up, once the treatment was written, I sometimes called the designer in and told him, "Listen, I need a place like this or like that..." And while I was writing, he would go and look. He brought me back photos or videos. And then I would take a quick trip and have a look. When I found a location I liked, I changed the screenplay so that I could use it. The same went for certain people I met. There were characters I discovered while looking for locations, and I changed the screenplay in order to fit them in.

– It's a film about the search for locations and people.

– Here's what happened. There were a hundred and twenty-six characters in the film. Out of those one hundred and twenty-six characters, the real professional actors, weren't more than ten or twelve.

How did this happen? About a year and a half before, before shooting *Una pura formalità,* in fact, it was two years before, I had written and prepared a film entirely set in Sicily, a spectacular film, complex, very beautiful, which couldn't be done because its cost was too high. While preparing that film, I did something that later turned out to be useful for this one.

I sent two of my assistants to Sicily to look for a provincial theater company, any kind at all, even the smallest, even a parish one, or a school one; I then went through all the companies with a fine-tooth comb and listed them. They found hundreds for me. And so I ended up with all this visual material, more than two thousand faces. Afterwards, it was decided that the film wouldn't be made; during the shooting of *this* film [*The Star Man*] I recycled that material. I found many of the characters in *The Star Man* in those files.

– So they already had at least a minimum of experience as actors...

– Yes, they had already done something. Sometimes even at an amateur level. But they had never acted on the stage of a big theater, nor in the movies. It turned out that I was able to use many of them. Naturally, I called them in again, made them go

through a new screening, but while looking for exteriors, sometimes I would meet other people whom I didn't know and who made such an impression on me that I immediately felt the need to change the screenplay and include them in the story, too. That happened several times.

– That is, using the availability of cinema as in the days of neorealism?

– Yes, in part. The fact that I controlled the screenplay, that I had to adjust and rewrite, was a constant voyage: we were always traveling. And we often had to change the screenplay. This control gave me the freedom that recalled the days of neorealism. One day I had to shoot a scene where, be-

Triumphant reception, at the Cannes Film Festival as well, for Giuseppe Tornatore's *Nuovo Cinema Paradiso/Cinema Paradiso,* and for the young actor Salvatore (Totò) Cascio, the irresistible kid who spends his time in the projection room of an old cinema.

Stopping in Naples, the aged father – to which Marcello Mastroianni gives moving force – mixes with a crowd watching a man threatening to jump from a building (*Stanno tutti bene/Everybody's Fine*).

fore Joe Morelli's camera, a young girl complains that no one in the village wants to marry her. No one wants to marry her because she has been accused of having slept with an American soldier. It was a difficult part. And I chose a non-professional theater actress. That morning, the actress didn't appear since she had been summoned by the Inspector of the Academy who wanted to offer her a teaching position. In fact, she had found the job of her life.

She called saying, "I'm sorry but I have to go there." And we found ourselves without an actress. So, I took one of the girls working as an extra and whose face had struck me. I called her and said, "Learn this by heart." I rewrote the dialogue adapting it to her dialect.

She learned it, we tried it a few times, and then acting, with all the embarassment she felt of having to recite her lines in front of her fellow townsmen laughing at her, teasing her, at one point she

burst out proudly and exploded, reciting her entire declamation with tremendous force, that force we see on the screen...

– *When there is this sort of availability, things can sometimes appear in front of you.*

– That's true, since when you're not locked into a rigid plan you're open, you become more sensitive to what's happening around you. When you go looking for a location, or in the morning while you're out shooting, you're aware that something might always just happen nearby that could be just perfect for the film. And you always have to be on the look out: knowing how to observe what's around you is very important. Then, you get the sensation you've just mentioned: even things, even reality, seem to come to you, to lend you a hand...

– *For example, Carmelo di Mazzarelli's appearance, the old man who was in Gianni Amelio's* Lamerica.

– Yes, by chance. He came to see me. I had seen his film a few months before; I recognized him immediately. He said to me, "Have me do something, I would so love to..." So I gave him a small part.

– *After his scene, the camera rises and we see the extraordinary sequence of the peasants with red flags that evokes the Portella della Ginestra sequence in Francesco Rosi's* Salvatore Giuliano.

– I must say that everyone thinks it's Portella, but that wasn't my intention since Portella della Ginestra wasn't a land occupation. It was May Day. Here, however, I wanted to show the great period of land occupation. Nevertheless, people, a hundred out of a hundred will say it's Portella, since the image of Portella della Ginestra is perhaps one of the most important sequences in the history of cinema. It is so fixed in the imagination that just seeing something that possibly evokes that image makes it immediately seem like an allusion to Rosi's film. It's something very curious.

– *People think, knowing the sequence, that it is indeed a homage to Rosi. In the film we also sense the influence of some of Pietro Germi's films.*

– In *The Star Man* there's a direct quote from Germi. In the end when Joe Morelli returns to the village for the girl and he goes to the movies, someone asks him, *"Are you Dottore* [an Italian term of respect] *Morelli?"* And he answers, *"I'm not a doctor."*

Germi used to say this all the time. Because he didn't like being called "Doctor." And every time someone called him that he used to say, "I'm not a doctor."

He had had a badge made that said, "I'm not a doctor." So when anyone called him Doctor, he pointed to the badge. It was something that had always struck me about this director's humility; I wanted to put it in my dialogue. But no one noticed, since no one knew the story.

– *I liked the choice of certain actors who had already played in some of your films, Leopoldo Trieste, Leo Gullotta...*

– There are several; it's a bit like working with your family. It becomes very easy to communicate what you want to some actors. They understand you so well that it's like working in a family.

One of the film's characters is even played by my father. He's not at all an actor, absolutely not. But for a long time I had wanted to have him play a small role... He plays the doctor, the doctor who offers Morelli a ride on his way to be paid for signing a death certificate.

– *Nanni Moretti also had his father act.*

– Many directors, when they can, ask members of their family. I think it's a way of feeling more at ease.

– *While you were writing the screenplay were you already thinking about the choice of the two leading actors, Joe Morelli and the*

young girl Beata? Two actors who had to be selected very carefully. Did you already have Sergio Castellitto in mind?

– Before writing the screenplay, that is, when I was still in the idea phase, I made an agreement with the producer based on this idea. At the time, I had two or three names in mind, among them Sergio Castellitto. Then, before even starting to write I saw them and Castellitto immediately seemed the most convincing. While telling him the story, I felt that he was sincerely attracted to the character. So, we did a screen test. We took a few shots. He convinced me. And I wrote the screenplay thinking of him.

When there are important characters, before writing, I always try to know who's going to play them.

It's hard for me to write without knowing who's going to play the part. And if I'm forced to write without knowing, then after choosing the actor, I have to rewrite, to make some adjustments. It's inevitable.

– *There's also a slight allusion to* Cinema Paradiso, *for example, the child who holds the* clapper *and looks a little like Salvatore Cascio.*

The splendid old age of Mastroianni in *Stanno tutti bene/Everybody's Fine.*

– Yes, a little. To tell the truth, this was again one of those things that happen by chance, which we were talking about before. One day in a village where we were filming, there was this child among the people who reminded me of Totò in *Cinema Paradiso,* though he especially reminded me of David Bennent, the child in *The Tin Drum.* If you look at him, they're identical. There wasn't a child holding the clapper in the screenplay since it was Morelli who was taking care of it. I then thought that perhaps, from time to time, Morelli could be helped by someone and at the end he would say to the child, "Here, here's three lire." Another example was the old man who speaks about the time he found himself before the execution squad when the Germans were going to shoot him... It was a true story, lived by that man himself. I knew him, I had him called over and asked him to tell his story. What he relates is completely true.

– *How did you discover Tiziana Lodato who plays the part of the young girl?*

– She was someone who had never done anything before. During our many auditions – and we did a lot – something happened that is frequent in America, and so my story even sounds a little untrue.

She had come to the auditon, not because she wanted to participate, but to accompany a friend who was an actress. I noticed her, I had her photographed, and in the end she's the one I chose. Of course, I called her and explained that it was a character that also had to play a few scenes that were a little... difficult for a young girl. There were some nude scenes, the scene when Morelli deflowers her. I had her read the screenplay, and since she was a minor, I had her read it to her parents, too. They talked a long time about it together, and in the end she accepted. But she filmed the sex scenes after she turned eighteen. I wanted her to be of age... She's a young girl from Catania. She's studying art history at the University. Now, she's planning on moving to Rome, but for now she's studying in Catania.

– *Thinking of making movies?*

– No. I explained to her that cinema – you have to

Philippe Noiret in Giuseppe Tornatore's episode "Il cane blu"/The Blue Dog from the film *La domenica special- mente/Especially on Sundays.* A series of poetic tales based on a screenplay by Tonino Guerra.

consider it a little like a game: you must never expect too much from movies; it's the worse thing you can do to not get anything in return. So, she's quite peaceful. She's very intelligent. But anyway, in the meantime, she's already made another film with Maurizio Ponzi.

– *In* The Star Man *she has an almost animal presence.*

– Yes. She's physical. Just what I was looking for to portray this character. Because in order to attract such an indifferent boorish man like Joe Morelli, we had to find an animal-like, carnal beauty. Morelli, without realizing it, falls in love with this girl because of an attraction to her skin, her smell, her flesh.

– *So, that's the description of a boor, someone who goes around trying to make a little money. At the worst, he's a crook?*

– Yes, a small-time crook, just like there were by

the thousands after World War II. To make ends meet, people came up with all kinds of things. He was one of the many.

– But at least he learns something during his trip.

– Yes, it's also the story of a great lesson in life that is learned unconsciously.

What I like about the character Morelli is that he's a boor, a crook, but he's a man who involuntarily, without realizing it, manages to discover himself; and he accomplishes this only by chance, only because he sets out to become a crook in a land where the most ancient collective dream is the desire that its story be told. That was my idea.

Sicilians perhaps have always hoped that someone could tell their story completely. And this never happened. They never felt their story had been told entirely. And that's why I showed the Sicilians just the opposite of how they're portrayed normally on the screen. Generally, Sicilians don't talk a lot in films. They're not open. Here, on the contrary, they tell everything. They tell everything because I think that deep down they're really like that.

– They need someone who will listen to them.

– Exactly. And perhaps, therefore, involuntarily, Morelli was the man they needed, the man just for them. And so Morelli discovers himself when he stumbles, by chance, across this unfulfilled collective dream, this eternal frustration of Sicily: the frustration of never having had its story told right to the end, the way it has always desired. This is what makes the character important. And I also like the fact that, at the end of the story, there is only one character who harshly avenges Morelli's swindling, among all those filmed by his camera, it's the dead man, it's the mafioso. Here we have the violent side of Sicily, the negative side, the aspect I don't like, that I detest. It's the only character who takes revenge. All the others, in fact, remain in Joe Morelli's limbo of newly acquired sensitivity. In my opinion, they represent the best side of Sicily, its ingenuousness, its desire to have its story told.

Beata, who probably represents all of them, expresses this positive desire to affirm herself through good, without resorting to violence: in the end she pays for everyone through her madness. Since Morelli is a crook, there's no way out: it's a dead end. But staying in Sicily is also a dead end because, for one thing, there is the State that doesn't respond to this kind of positive dream.

The corporal, for example, when he finds himself confronted in the end with the crook's lawful punishment, surrenders to the pressure of the Mafia and they go, he and the prosecutor, leaving Morelli to the Mafia.

And thus this young girl with her honest and true dream, can only touch what Pirandello called the wrong chord. That is why she goes insane in the end.

Some feel that this dramatic denouement is forced. For me, it was the only probable destiny for this character. There couldn't be a "happy ending." It would have been artificial since Morelli, in any case, even though unconsciously, had made a mockery of the genuineness of these people.

– The film can be understood on different levels.

– Yes, for example Lietta Tornabuoni, who really liked the film, remarked that one of the levels that I had tucked in quite well between the lines was related to politics. She understood the film as a metaphor for politicians.

She saw it as a story of the promises made by politicians to a country that for fifty years has tried to improve itself without ever managing to. As the eternal promise of politics that can never honor its commitments and has either placed the country in the grips of schizophrenia, or surrendered it to retrograde, reactionary and violent forces. On the other hand, Tullio Kezich asked other questions. "Perhaps he means that historically cinema has failed in the great plan to help improve Sicily. Because, perhaps cinema has never succeeded, except in some exceptional cases, in telling this country's story in a way that would help Sicily to redeem itself." Therefore, almost like the eternal failure of all means of communication.

These are various levels, all very interesting.

– But in terms of failure of the means of communication, I don't think it's possible to imagine the "non-failure." Cinema can only give one side of reality, one particular testimony. This was what

Sciascia was saying when he wrote that no film, except perhaps Salvatore Giuliano, *which was the one that had come closest to it, had ever succeeded in telling Sicily's story.*

– Yes, absolutely. In my opinion, five films have succeeded in relating something important, *La terra trema, Salvatore Giuliano,* a few films by Germi, *The Leopard.*

But, as you can see, they are very few.

– Elio Petri's *A ciascuno il suo?*

– Yes. *A ciascuno il suo.* But there, the fact that it was based on a text by Sciascia is important. *Todo modo* is even stranger. We have Sciascia's contribution, but Petri already presents a personal analysis in this film. He begins by taking Sciascia's book as a pretext for holding a type of "palace" trial against Italian politics, almost by predicting the collapse of the great political parties. It is a visionary film that

has completely disappeared from circulation. No one can see it. No video cassettes exist. Television never shows it. *Cadaveri eccellenti* by Rosi has disappeared too, another important film.

– *The film set in Sicily that you were preparing, the one that was so expensive, will it ever be made?*

– I don't think so. It was a film about the great popular myth of politics. A film on Italy, told through Sicily, during a time when everyone believed that they could only attain a better life through politics. A great utopia.

Fifty years later, people believe that this has been lost forever. Because in Italy now the big problem is that people no longer believe in politics.

No one believes anymore that politics is a means of creating a more just society, more modern, more equitable. This is the big problem. And I don't think it's a problem that's limited only to Italy. The collapse of ideologies has caused the collapse of confidence in politics as a way of building a democracy.

This is very serious. Very dangerous. So, I thought that telling everyone how – barely forty, forty-five years ago – everyone believed in it... I thought that this was important. And I imagined this story about popular upheavals, great collective dreams. And it was a film about the great masses, through the friendship between two young people. One, politically prepared, very committed, the other completely disoriented.

The impostor arrested. Sergio Castellitto in Giuseppe Tornatore's *L'uomo delle stelle/The Star Man.*

And through this friendship we live the most important historical and political moments in Sicily's history: from the debarkation of the Americans in 1943 right up to July 8, 1960, when the

The impossible shooting in Sicily, of its men and its women, by Joe Morelli's camera (Sergio Castellitto) in Giuseppe Tornatore's *L'uomo delle stelle/The Star Man.*

Tramboni government ordered strikers in several cities in Italy to be shot.

Here, politics is truly the beginning and the end of everything. Why couldn't we make it? It was a highly spectacular film that called for thirty, forty thousand extras. The heroes were two young people, so that meant we couldn't choose very well-known actors. We were unsuccessful. What was more, according to the producers, there were too many red flags. They told me that no one was interested anymore in films about politics. I wasn't able to get it together and I'm afraid I never will.

– Perhaps the main quality of The Star Man *is that, as spectators, we can understand the film on a basic level, a beautiful love story; or we can find more serious matter for reflection. One point: not all spectators agree about the succession of all the faces at the end of the movie.*

– Do you know how I got that idea? At the beginning of the film Joe Morelli is a totally insensitive man, he couldn't care less about what the people are saying to him. He's interested in the thousand five hundred lire, he only thinks about eating and chasing after women. That's it. And his film is as insensitive as he is. Nothing remains on the film. And I thought that at the end of the story, even if nothing remained on the film, in his mind, yes.

So, I made this double exposure, as if instead of on his film, the images were recorded upon this new-found sensitivity.

Only, maybe I could have made this sequence a little shorter. For me, the faces that he takes with him are the positive element in my ending that would otherwise have been completely pessimistic. In the end, all these people whom he takes with him are basically positive figures and he takes them with him thanks to his newly acquired conscience.

Therefore, for me, there is still hope. The fact that he says to the girl in the psychiatric hospital, "If you like I'll come back, we can talk about what you think," is for me like an open window.

– I imagine that Morelli returned, from time to time, to see Beata.

– Yes, since in any case, when a person like him discovers love, and also the way he tells Beata that he has fallen in love with her, we understand he has acquired something new in terms of sensitivity. Perhaps those who think that I could have made the end a little shorter are right. But other than that, I really think it was the best possible ending.

Giuseppe Tornatore discussing with Leo Gullotta and Marcello Mastroianni in the Neapolitan episode of *Stanno tutti bene/Everybody's Fine*, the odyssey of a Sicilian father on a trip to visit his children, from the South to the North of Italy, from Palermo to Torino.